Buck Taylor's

Practical Guide To Catching More Crappie

by Buck Taylor

Outdoor Skills Bookshelf
P.O. Box 111501
Nashville, TN 37211

This book is dedicated to Harold and Claire.
No man could love his children more than I
do the two of them.

Contents

General description of the two species of Crappie, their habits and habitat; illustrations showing the differences between the two species of Black and White Crappie; spawning details.

Roadblocks to successful crappie fishing; reasons why many anglers come home without fish.

Five positive methods for taking crappie consistently; description of miscellaneous seasonal methods; details on constructing and locating underwater fish attractors; tips and comments on depthfinders and their use.

How to catch crappie in every month of the year; methods used by three professional guides whose successes are documented with results year-round; rivers and creeks; man-made impoundments and reservoirs; how to catch suspended crappie; miscellaneous tips on tackle, bait and water conditions.

Detailed explanations of the most productive procedures for crappie fishing success in Winter, Spring, Summer and Fall.

A look at the use of depthfinders and how they increase your ability to bring in more crappie in every season; ten clear illustrations taken from actual graph paper which show crappie in their typical locations during various times of the year.

Secret to fast, easy cleaning of crappie; recipes for delicious eating with all the trimmings.

Preface

Crappie fishermen are my kind of people.

Show me a man or woman who enjoys crappie fishing and I'll show you one who enjoys the fun and takes the results home to the skillet. To me, that's what it's all about: wholesome fun outdoors on the water and good eating as a result of the effort.

After many years of fishing for fun in several states, my career as an accountant/financial whiz took me to Kentucky where the crappie are both big and plentiful. A few more years in the pencil-pushing business and I revolted. Corporate politics and the routine of bowing and scraping to one who by virtue of his position in the Company somehow merited subordinate behavior was a bit more than I could swallow. I became a full-time outdoor journalist, hunting and fishing seven days each week, spending nights and unusual hours at the typewriter preparing articles for the various magazines. My "fall from Grace" by telling the business world to go fly a big one was met with dismay by friends and loved ones. But I caught a lot of fish. And we sure ate well on a regular basis.

I also learned some pretty neat secrets and tricks from the experts regarding how to fill a stringer or a freezer with crappie. Interviews, personal experience trying out ideas before committing them to paper, and the sheer joy received from going on the lake alone and returning with an ice chest filled with fish, was incentive enough. I became an addict with a cheap habit. Crappie fishing was both relaxing and rewarding. It saved the grocery bills, fed the family tasty meals on a predictable schedule every month of the year, and gave me a secret sense of accomplishment returning to the dock with a dozen or two pounds of tablefare when others had tried and come back empty.

Even with the most serious effort possible, one cannot class the crappie as a "sport fish" similar to tarpon, smallmouth bass and freshwater stripers. They don't jump, strip off line in mad dashes of power, or break fragile line used in attempts to set records. They just feed regularly and allow themselves to be caught easily by those of us who like hot fish and hushpuppies from time to time. Maybe that's why *the crappie happens to be the most popular fish for anglers nationwide*, despite all the articles I had to write about bass, stripers and numerous other gamefish. Those articles were written because the editors wanted them, and they were the ones who signed the paychecks for my words.

But when no article assignments were pending, or when we simply wanted a mess of fish for the table, crappie became the object of my attention. Fortunately, I was able to generate enough articles on crappie fishing from the magazine folks to spend at least a goodly part of my time doing something I liked.

This book offers you a chance to share in the

times and lessons I have had on the water catching crappie. You may have found a "new secret" for catching them that I have missed. The species lends itself to a wide variety of methods for success. But I can promise the following pages will give you ideas and suggestions to apply to your own waters which are proven fish-getters. There's even a section on methods for catching crappie in *every* month of the year.

After leaving the business world, I spent several years as a professional fishing guide. Most of the chaps who paid for the fun were after bass or stripers. But when I got somebody who simply wanted to have fun and take home several pounds of fillets, we went crappie fishing.

There's no magic required to catch crappie. All you have to do is understand the fish, learn about its habits, and do a bit of clear thinking on the subject of water conditions. You are about to read those things, and my goal is to present the lifestyle of this fish in such a manner that you will be able to go to the lake or river and have FUN!

Buck Taylor

ACKNOWLEDGMENTS

The author wishes to express his thanks and appreciation to the following individuals and Companies who contributed, in a variety of ways, to the research and production of this book:

BETTS TACKLE LTD.
Susan Bibler, JUHL ASSOCIATES
Larry Colombo, TECHSONIC INDUSTRIES, INC.
Lanny Deal
Rex Gerlack, DIAWA CORPORATION
Carl Hamilton
Joe Hughes, REBEL BAITS
IGLOO CORPORATION
Paul Johnson, BERKLEY CORPORATION
Bob Lancina
Tom Mann
Bob Maxwell
Steve McCadams
PLANO, INC.
Wayne, Lynda & Teddy
SHELDONS', INC.
TEMPRESS CORPORATION
John & Mae Toft, Zimbabwe AFRICA
Gary VanderMause, UNCLE JOSH BAIT COMPANY
Mike Vierzba, RYOBI AMERICA CORPORATION
Ben West, Jr.
ZEBCO CORPORATION

Buck Taylor's

Practical Guide To Catching More Crappie

Crappie are the Number One fish in popularity nationwide today. (Photo courtesy Tennessee Wildlife Resources Agency)

1

The Quarry

In my copy of the book "Sport Fishing USA" put out by the U.S. Department of the Interior, there is an article on crappie which lists over 50 different names people use when referring to this species! Even with such a wide variety of local identities all across the country, crappie come only in two basic flavors: Black and White.

The White Crappie, *Pomoxis annularis,* is fairly widespread throughout the States, partially due to its ability to tolerate minor pollution and turbidity in the water. The White Crappie has six dorsal and six anal spines; the dark specks on his sides are roughly arranged in vertical bars. Females lay from 3,000 to 15,000 eggs during spawning time. When small, the White Crappie has a definite preference for insects and plankton. As it matures, its diet shifts to fish, primarily gizzard shad. Average weight is about one pound, but two and three-pounders are not uncommon.

The Black Crappie, *Pomoxis nigromaculatus*, is found from southern Canada all the way down

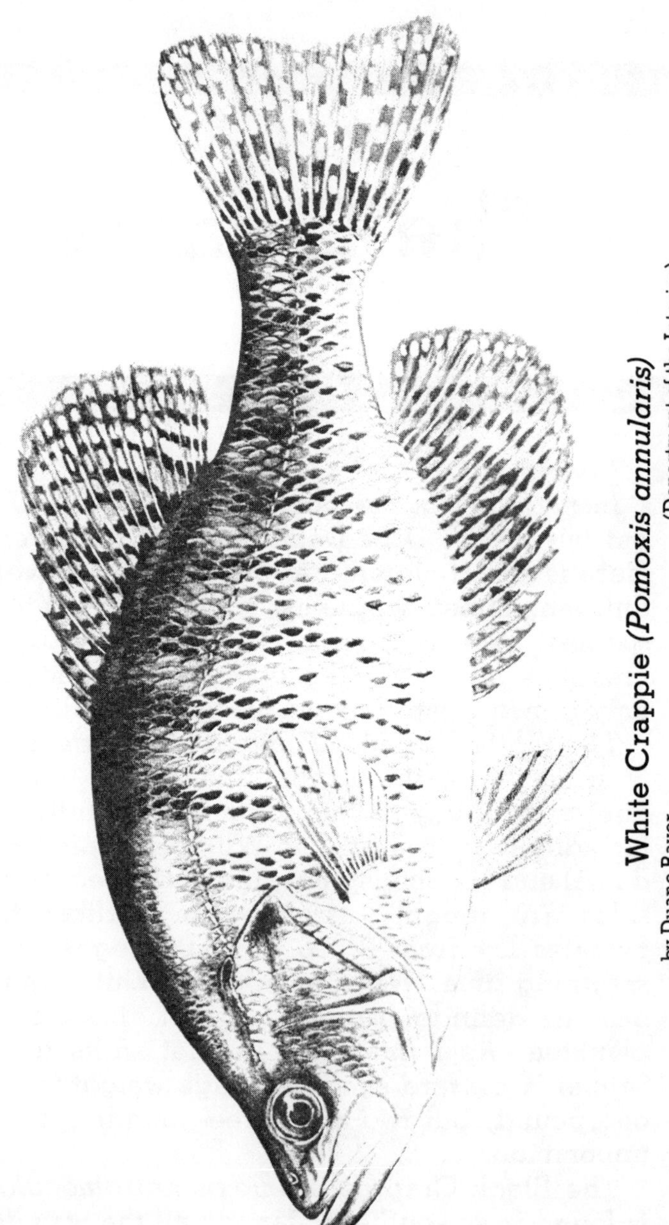

White Crappie *(Pomoxis annularis)*
(Department of the Interior)
by Duane Raver

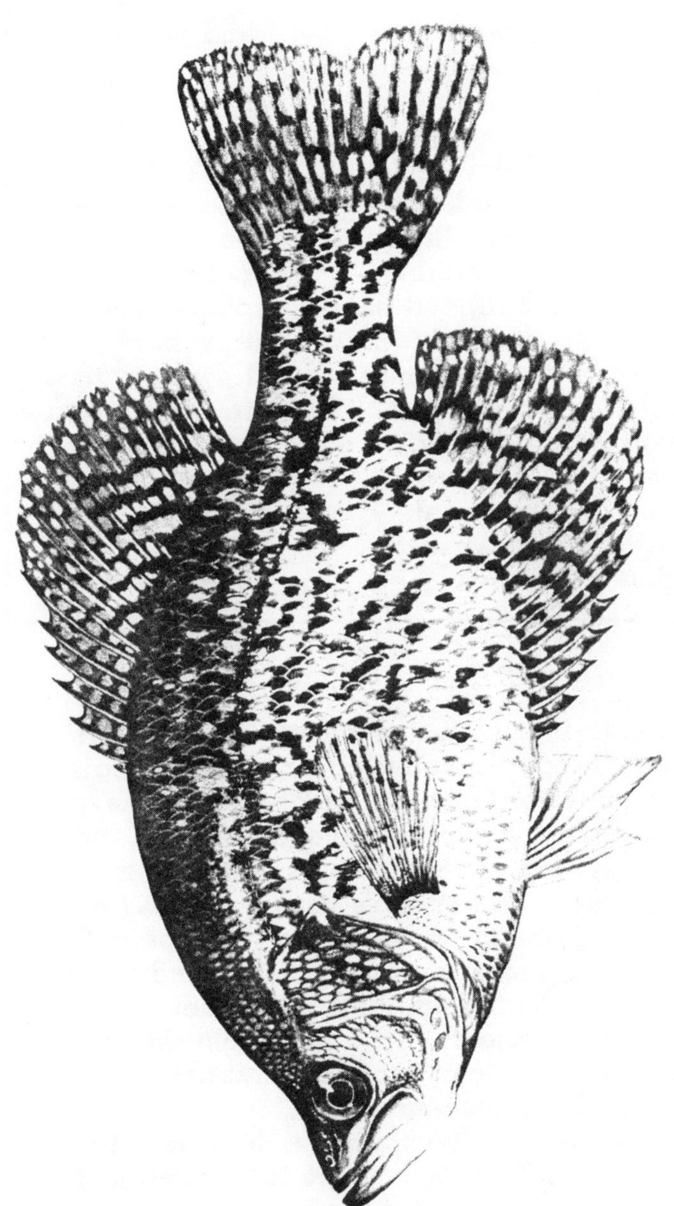

Black Crappie (*Pomoxis nigromaculatus*)
(Department of the Interior)

by Duane Raver

bachelor	goggle-eye	sand perch
bachelor perch	goggle-eye perch	shad
bachelor shad	goldring	silver bass
banklick	grass bass	silver perch
banklick bass	John Demon	speckled bass
barfish	lake bass	speckled perch
bigfin bass	Lake Erie bass	speck
bitterhead	lamplighter	spotted perch
bride perch	Millpond bass	spotted trout
bridge perch	newlight	straw bass
calico	papermouth	strawberry bass
calico bass	perch	strawberry perch
calico bream	razorback	suckley perch
campbellite	roach	sun perch
chinquapin	sac-a-lait	tin mouth
chinquapin perch	rockfish	tin perch
Dolly Varden	sago	white perch

into Florida. It prefers the clean, quiet waters with a good bit of vegetative cover, and has a low tolerance for water pollution. Black Crappie have six to nine spines in their dorsal and anal fins, and the black specks on their sides are scattered without pattern. This species usually doesn't attain a weight much in excess of one pound, although there are exceptions where conditions are ideally suited for them. Its primary diet is fish, but it will take insects, crawfish, mollusks and shrimp. The female can produce anywhere from 20,000 to 50,000 eggs annually.

Both fish are similar in shape; however, the Black has a more concave shape to its head and upper back. Basic coloration is silver with green

This floating tree was snagged on a cable securing the boat dock. It held a great many crappie within its branches.

to dark olive blotches and black specks. Both species tend to overpopulate small bodies of water and fare better in waters offering some degree of movement as opposed to being stagnant. The same fishing methods, tackle and baits are used successfully on both Black and White Crappie.

Crappie are slow-growing fish with relatively short lifespans. A four-year-old is mature, and an eight-year-old is indeed ancient. Food availability is the controlling factor in growth.

When water temperatures climb into the

Crappie help build many memorable hours on the water when the kids get to join in on the fun.

mid-60's, crappie move into the shallows in-preparation for spring spawning. They are the earliest spawners of the sunfish family, and do so in deeper water than the others (typically from 3 to 10 feet). They occasionally spawn in water only inches deep, and in one recorded instance a female was documented as having layed 158,000 eggs!

Spawning usually takes place when the water temperature is between 65 and 68 degrees. The males go into the shallower water first, sporting their darker mating colors, and fan out small dish-shaped depressions in the bottom. They select areas with hard bottom when possible, as silt which could cover over the nest is a definite hazzard to the survival of the eggs. The males remain on or near the nestsites until a willing female comes along. After mating, the male remains there to guard the nest. The eggs hatch in 3 to 15 days depending on the water temperatures.

Once the fry hatch, they become a favorite food for the parents. This is why crappie fishing often goes in cycles. When conditions permit an exceptionally good hatch, the surviving fish become the dominant year class in the body of water. There are so many of them that in the years to come they devour huge quantities of fry and decimate populations in those years. Only after the dominant year class dies out will the overall population get back into balance. Another large spawn survives and the cycle starts over.

Crappie fry grow to three-or-four-inch size in the first year. They feed more heavily in the second year, reaching the five-to-seven-inch length. They hit the eight-to-ten-inch mark in the third year, maturing at about 12 inches in the fourth.

These fish are most active in the spring and feed heavily in connection with spawning activities. However, they take live bait and small artificials all year around. They follow definite movement patterns, or migrations, and their location can be predicted with very good accuracy in practically any month of the year. The fish have large, but very fragile mouths, making it necessary to use caution when hooking them to prevent tearing the mouth tissue and losing the fish.

Crappie are calculated to be the number one fish in America in popularity among anglers, based upon man-hours devoted to catching them. Truly a Fish for All Seasons and one for all people to enjoy, crappie provide countless hours of pleasure for American fishermen. On the pages which follow, tips, techniques and proven patterns will be explained for taking home more of these great fish in every month of the year.

Crappie definitely are *NOT* a one-season fish! (Photo courtesy John Phillips)

2

Misconceptions
Roadblocks to Success

Funny how we go through life forming opinions based on things we are told, or by looking only surface deep at the events around us. I wasted a lot of time in Junior High School waiting to find a girl who brought her own blanket to the hayrides we had on weekends. Girls like that, I had been told, really wanted to have "fun," while all the others simply went along to toast marshmallows and sing songs around the bonfire. I went through a whole summer of weekends with non-blanket-carrying girls, and never questioned or tested their unwillingness to do a little smooching under the moonlight. The final hayride of the summer was quite different. This time, my date showed up with a blanket, and I figured things were finally going my way.

An entire summer spent wanting to kiss a girl and having to settle for burnt marshmallows is likely to give a teenager a rejection complex. I was so excited when my date showed up with the required equipment, I tried to kiss her as soon as the wagon started rolling along the back roads.

Open water fishing is a new twist to the majority of crappie anglers, but it works year-round. (Photo courtesy TWRA)

"No thank you," she said curtly, turning her head away. "I'm not like *all* these other girls who do that sort of thing every weekend. I just like the part where we sit around the fire to eat and sing."

Why many of us are so willing to take advice at face value without question, I really don't know. But in crappie fishing, failure to experiment a little on your own often prevents success.

It's doubtful anyone who has fished for crappie more than four or five times has failed to experience at least one day of less-than-spectacular success. This is true even if all their efforts were made during the spawning season when the action is "always" excellent. Sometimes the reasons for not catching hefty stringers of crappie are quite legitimate. Four-foot whitecaps on the lake make it tough to position the boat on target, for example.

Most of the time, however, we fail to bring in braggin' size catches because of non-existent groundrules we impose upon ourselves. Someone tells us, and we believe them, the fish are chomping minnows in the shallows at four-foot depths. We climb into our waders or fire the boat engine and head for the shallow area our pal suggested. There we spend three or four fruitless hours wagging minnows all over the place four feet beneath the surface. We get tired, lose patience and head home blaming the barometer, or all the other boats in the area doing the same thing. What we overlooked was the fact nobody told the fish they had to stay at the four-foot level for another 24 hours until we arrived. And since our pal *did* tell us to fish at that depth, we figured if it worked yesterday for him, it should work today for us.

I remember a four-day trip to Kentucky Lake years ago when we hit it perfectly, our arrival coinciding with hot action in the brush along the shoreline. Crappie were being hauled in right and left by fishermen dunking minnows only 18 inches below a float into the brush. Pretty fantastic action, and the kind of stuff spring vacations are scheduled around, at least hopefully so.

The second day there, we ate a hearty breakfast, took our time getting our gear into the boat, and finally shoved off for the section of shore which had produced beautifully for us the day before. We were so confident of our success we actually discussed the "problem" we were going to have when our big Igloo cooler became filled with fish! Two hours later, thoughts about running out of room for our catch were far removed

Knowing where they will be and trying different methods will produce rewards like this. (Photo courtesy TWRA)

from our minds. Two small crappie don't take up excessive space in an ice chest.

Eventually, my hook wandered around part of the brush and became snagged. I tried to shake it off, but in the process the float came off the line. Fortunately, it sailed back in my direction, and I was able to lean over the side of the boat to retrieve it. Thus distracted, I failed to notice the hook had come dislodged and the split shot on the line took it to the bottom. Realizing what had happened, I tried to lift the rig straight upwards in an attempt at not getting snagged again. Getting the hook back up through the brush proved no problem, and the big crappie that had swallowed it sure brightened the day!

We worked a 200-yard stretch of shoreline the rest of the day, dropping minnows into the brush and letting them go to the bottom (about five feet). All you had to do was raise the pole up a few inches to tighten the line and lift the bait off bottom, and you had a fish. We lost plenty of hooks in the brush, but we filled the ice chest, too!

Probably the worst bit of misinformation crappie fishermen suffer comes from the generally-accepted idea these fish are primarily seasonal. Anglers go to the lakes in large numbers during March, April and May, depending upon where they live, trying to capitalize on the fun during the spawning activity. The fishing is easy; the catches are plentiful. Everybody loves it. When the crappie move back away from the shoreline, the vast majority of fishermen put away their minnow buckets for another 12 months.

Crappie are more predictable, and can be caught with more dependability, in August than in either March, April or May!

This point was demonstrated clearly to me by a good friend, Carl Hamilton, years ago fishing on Kentucky Lake. Carl is one of the most successful crappie fishermen I have ever known, and makes a habit of coming back to the dock with fish when others come in empty. He does it in every month of the year, too.

I nursed my old Ford pickup from Nashville to the west side of Kentucky Lake one July afternoon when the temperatures were hitting the 100-degree mark. Carl was waiting for me at Sportsman's Lodge & Marina on Jonathan Creek, boat and bait ready. I had been telling myself for two and one-half hours behind the wheel on the road that this routine was a waste of time, sweating profusely in the air-conditionless truck. Carl's reassuring smile, plus the cold beer I opened when finished driving, made me feel better. We left the dock about four o'clock in the afternoon. I could see heat waves shimmering above Carl's boat engine, even before he cranked it.

As it turned out, Carl's expertise and knowledge of crappie fishing did more to change my ideas on summer crappie fishing than could have all the alternatives possible. We were back at the dock before sunset with an ice chest literally filled to the brim with nice crappie. He had taken me straight to the old river channel, found the shoulder and drop-off with his depthfinder, and proceeded to teach me the highly-effective procedure he uses for "bottom bumping" with a double-hook rig. I was amazed. I was even more amazed when he did the same thing on each of the following two days, both of which featured wilting temperatures near the top of the thermometer at the bait shop. Never again, would I consider crappie fishing limited to the springtime spawning runs!

I have heard crappie fishermen say the fish simply won't bite in cold weather, opting to suspend somewhere in the lake and ignore the rest of the world until spring. It's true the fish slow down their activity when water temperatures drop, but the poor things couldn't survive the winter if they didn't eat something. This excuse for not fishing in the cold months may smack of "rationalization" in order to avoid cold noses and frozen fingertips on the part of the fisherman! You'll find wintertime crappie fishing is a test of your patience, and a test of your ability to detect faint taps on the line, however.

Crappie in cold water neither chase a bait nor grab it with authority when it passes under their little pointed noses. Typically, they will gently suck the bait into their mouth and sit there, as if resting before they have to swallow it. "Sport" never enters the picture for winter crappie fishermen. Those of us who brave the elements for a mess of cold-weather crappie are simply hungry for a mess of tasty fish. And crappie in cold water do indeed taste better than at any other time of year. The meat is more firm, also.

Far too many crappie fishermen believe minnows are the only bait to use in filling a stringer. I have found times when minnows seem to be the *best* bait to use, but jigs and small spinners were producing also. Normally, when you find active crappie, they will hit either or both. Artificials are easier and less expensive in the long run; they also are faster when the action takes on the character of "every cast success," since you don't have to stop to put on another minnow every time

Crappie on ultra-light tackle maximize the fun.

you catch a fish. I usually take along both. Depending on the situation, I'll wag a natural live bait down where they live until I find the fish. Then, providing the action gets hot and heavy, I'll switch to a jig or small spinner. Even while I'm exercising a minnow on one pole, I may be casting tiny artificials on another. This not only helps materially in finding the depth where the fish are holding, but also increases my chances by multiplying the cubic feet of water I'm covering.

The final misconception crappie fishermen

Crappie often hang around docks and piers; fish right next to the posts and pilings. (Photo courtesy Louisiana Wildlife & Fisheries Commission)

often must overcome is that the fish follow the same routine every day. Please remember, anything which is cold-blooded and has scales on it will be genuinely affected by various stimuli provided by its environment. A drop in temperature (even a slight one), a change in the water level courtesy of the dudes controlling the dam gates, an overcast day following a week of sunshine, or even heavy rainfall, will cause a reaction and a change of behaviour in fish.

The one thing I'm going to try hardest to show you in this book is the importance of staying out of a set pattern with your crappie fishing. When you go to the lake or river with a pre-conceived plan for catching your fish, the only times you'll be successful are those days when the fish happen to be following the same script. Witness experiences of your own when everything was "perfect" according to plan, but you spent hours on end trying to boat a few small fish. They *should* have been on the bank spawning in shallow water. They took everything in sight at eight-foot depths yesterday afternoon; they *should* do the same this morning. Lucky Bob caught his limit in two hours just 20 yards off Turkey Point yesterday. He fished on the righthand side of the point on the drop-off leading towards the beach. The crappie *should* be there again at daylight and we *should* kill 'em. But we don't kill 'em; we don't even catch a half-dozen fish. Why not?

The answer is as simple as the solution. The fish obviously have moved. They're still feeding, and we can still catch them like gangbusters. But we didn't move with them, so we spent the day exercising minnows in water which held no crappie.

It's almost a sure bet the fish were only a few yards away from us, but just out of range for our limited efforts to pay off in edible dividends. Moving around, changing depths, or simply changing bait size could easily have turned a lousy day into a great one.

Successful crappie fishing can be compared to making love. If you go about it in the same mechanical, predictable manner every time, you're going to miss out on a whole lot of fun.

Learn five basic methods for taking crappie and you can catch them almost every time out. (Photo courtesy Bob Dennie)

3

Techniques That Work

Crappie are one of the most cooperative species of fish in fresh water, providing countless hours of fun and a mindboggling tonnage of tablefare for anglers all across the country. Every member of the clan, from Grandma and Gramps down the line to the tiny tykes who require miniature-size life preservers, can and do catch crappie. Equipment needs are modest and inexpensive. You don't need a sleek water machine pushed by a monster engine at eye-watering speeds, and crappie really don't care whether you catch them with a fancy graphite outfit or a cane pole. They routinely take a great variety of small jigs and lures, and they sink store-bought bobbers by the tens of millions annually for live bait anglers. It is doubtful even the people at IBM could calculate accurately the number of hushpuppies consumed every year to accompany hot platters of fried crappie.

One of the really neat things about catching crappie is the number of ways you can do it successfully. Conversely, one of the mysteries to the casual observer is why crappie fishermen so often employ only a single method for filling a stringer, even on days when that particular approach is not producing well.

Listed below are several proven techniques for catching crappie. I make no claims the list is all-inclusive. But I am willing to bet good money you can improve you year-round catch if you will master some or most of these methods. The real key to success is learning several approaches that work, and *using all of them.* Nobody hits a homerun every time they go to bat, but if you go to the lake or river with a variety of methods in your gameplan, your chances of filling the ice chest are increased tremendously.

Basic Bottom Bumping

If listed in order of importance, this technique surely deserves the Number One slot. It works in every month of the year: hot, cold, or in-between. Master this one, and you have a technique that rarely fails.

Several things contribute to the success of this method. For starters, you present your bait at two different depths simultaneously, both of which are near the bottom. Crappie are structure-oriented, as are most fish, and this technique allows you to "feel" the structure you are working. Additionally, the nature of the fish you seek to catch makes working the bottom layer of water more productive than any other. Even when warming water temperatures drive the crappie into the shallows, they go with irregular intensity; large numbers of the fish remain in the deeper

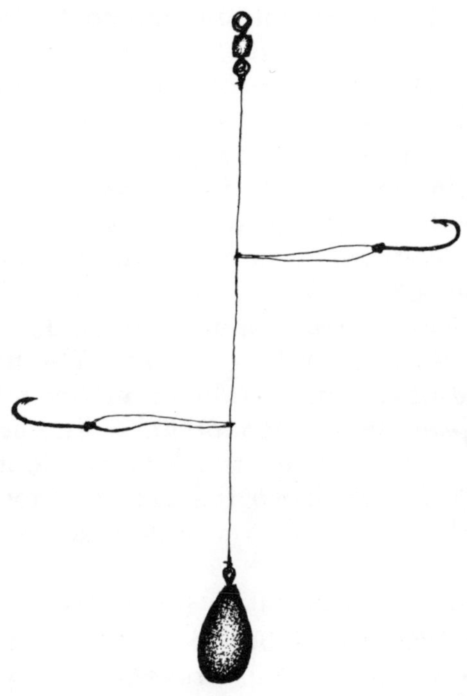

water, near bottom and are highly catchable at those times.

The terminal rig used in bottom bumping is made up with a pair of 2/0 thin wire hooks and a one-ounce bell sinker. You can make these yourself, or purchase them ready-made in a great many bait shops. Some places offer dual-hook crappie rigs constructed with the lead weight positioned between the two hooks; often dressing the rig with small spinner blades and florescent beads. If the weight is positioned beneath the two hooks, you merely bounce it on bottom to keep both baited hooks slightly above the real estate; if the weight is placed between the hooks, you must reel in aproximately a foot of line after letting the lead strike bottom to accomplish the same thing. When fishing a drop-off or ever-changing bottom configuration, the rig featuring a lead sinker below both hooks makes life easier. Both style rigs work to give excellent results.

Making your own bottom-bumping rig requires only a few simple items. You will need a barrel swivel, some 30-pound monofilament line, and of course, the hooks and lead sinker. Tie the sinker to the end of the line. Eighteen inches above the sinker, fashion a simple loop knot. Another 18 inches above that, tie the second loop knot. Perhaps two feet above the second knot, attach the swivel. The weight on bottom keeps the line taut.

The heavy mono plays two roles. It is stiff enough to allow the loops to stand out away from the vertical main line, preventing a constant tangle. And it is strong enough to allow a muscular upwards heave on the line when you're hung up on brush without breaking. In most cases, thin wire hooks will straighten out before 30-pound mono snaps.

The technique employed in putting this double-hook rig to work for you is reasonably easy. All it takes is a bit of practice to get the "feel" of what you are doing. The fish will do the rest. And your stringer weight will profit greatly, not only with crappie, but also with bass, sauger, catfish, bream and anything else cruising the bottom layer of your local waters that happens to be hungry for minnows or jigs. (The eye of a jig will

Crappie take a number of baits and lures; the key is giving them what they want at the right depth. (Photo courtesy TWRA)

thread over those two loops in the line with equal ease of the 2/0 wire hooks.) Keep the slack out of your line at all times.

The rod or pole you employ when using this bottom-bumping technique is optional. The best outfit I have seen is one made on a small scale by a gentleman named Dutch Owen in Fulton, Kentucky. It features a telescoping fiberglass pole with a fine wire imbedded in the tip for extra sensitivity. A line-keeper reel is attached to the butt end, allowing one to adjust the amount of line used from tip to bottom, eliminating excess slack in the line. Fly rods, cane poles with simple line-

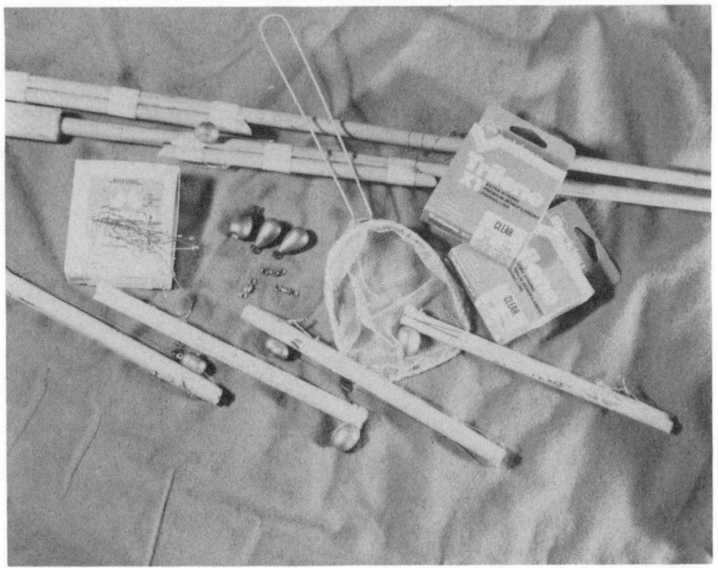

You can make your own double-hook rigs for tightline fishing, or purchase the ready-made ones from bait stores when available.

keepers taped on, spinning rods in the six or seven-foot class, or various types of fiberglass bream poles will all work satisfactorily.

The procedure is quite easy for using this rig. Enough line is let out of the reel or line-keeper to allow the lead sinker to reach bottom. Just as the name of the technique implies, you "bounce" the bottom with the sinker, keeping the two baited hooks a short distance above ground. With minimum practice, you will learn to feel the structure below, eventually gaining finesse sufficient to distinguish between a mud bottom and one made up of harder stuff. You learn to "feel" a stump or brush pile within minutes of your first attempt at bottom-bumping. And when you feel the structure below, you know you're in the right pew for catching crappie. You search for the structure with your depthfinder, zero in with your rig.

You will catch more crappie near the bottom than at any other depth if you average their elevation over 12 months of the year. Using two hooks at different depths allows you to compensate for the small variances they select from day to day. Quite often, you will capture two crappie at the same time on this rig, although that's not really the purpose in having dual hooks. Sometimes, 18 inches in depth can make the difference between feeding the Preacher supper and trying to tell him the damn fish weren't biting without cursing.

Bottom bumping works every month of the year if you select the correct area to bump around on. We'll cover that in detail when we get to the chapter on Practical Applications. For now, I want you to remember this technique and try it the next time out on the water. It works like a charm to put crappie in your boat. Of all the methods, tight-lining has to be the most consistent.

Constructing Habitat

If Mother Nature and Lady Luck strapped on roller skates and became co-captains of the Kansas City Bombers, they still would need a little help from their friends. Fallen trees, stump rows and other wooden havens for crappie have the habit of decaying when left underwater for a few years. Natural habitat for these fish eventually disolves and disappears. And looking at fishing pressure for this popular species, coupled with

When the water is down in winter, knowledgeable fishermen make the effort to build fish attractors which pay real dividends later. (Photo courtesy TWRA)

the availability of topographic maps, you can bet your anchor rope you're not going to be the only hopeful on the lake who knows where the remnants of the original stuff is located.

Constructing crappie habitat, or "beds," is a popular pastime for the chaps who ignore the freezing weather and muddy bottom during the low-water winter months. Rivers and lakes often shrink a bit around the first of the year, allowing us the opportunity to see with our eyes what our depthfinders have been trying to show us all summer. It's an ideal time to build brush piles, stake beds or various types of fish attractors. It's not the easiest of chores, especially in the cold temperatures, but if you keep reminding yourself of the great fun you'll be having there in about 90 days, it somehow seems less like work.

I've seen guys on my local lake hauling enough brush and small timber to imitate the Chicago fire if they had a quart of kerosene. The majority of it was hidden with great care out in the depths and secretly marked by lining up a variety of land-marks on shore. A big part of it probably never attracted a crappie, either. Putting out crappie beds is one of the best ways to insure yourself of a private "honey hole" later in the year. Sinking the stuff at random in the lake usually is a waste of good pulpwood.

Crappie follow definite routes when they move or migrate from one part of the lake to another. Underwater structure is the only Rand McNally available to them, so their roads and Interstates take the form of river and creek channels, old road beds, ditches, drop-offs, points and even flooded fence lines. Putting your brush piles in a semi-flat, structureless area is like opening a restaurant six miles off the main road. You can have great food and clean restrooms, but you're not gonna have to worry about parking space.

Plant your fish attractors on or near natural changes in the bottom which crappie will remain in contact with when they move about. The only exception to this is when you're trying to "doctor" a spot for the spring spawning run, as crappie go a bit nutso when they charge the banks to mate. You could probably stick your cane pole in the shallows at this time and some lovesick male would hang around there for a few days. But for the remaining 10 months of the year, your best

Sinking brush piles like this generates genuine fun and heavy stringers. (Photo courtesy TWRA)

bet is to sink your crappie condos on the edge of channels or drop-offs in about 20 feet of water. Try to figure out the probable water level during the time you'll be using the bed, and keep the top of your brush pile about 10 or 15 feet below the surface at that time.

Any number of tricks will work for crappie attractors. In late December, you can prowl the neighborhood picking up discarded Christmas trees. Attach a concrete block to the base and drop them into the water. They will stand upright, providing good cover for crappie-attracting minnows, and due to the upwards sweep of the branches, your hook won't be easily snagged when you cast or work live bait around them.

A bale of hay or two, especially alfalfa or Timothy, will make an excellent crappie attractor. Sink them with adequate weight, as hay bales like to float in some lakes, and if not floating they seem to enjoy moving around on the bottom with the current, making it tough to find them again.

Cedar trees, willow branches or practically any variety of brush in the woods will turn the trick for you, providing you locate the stuff along natural routes crappie will travel.

Stake beds, usually 1x3 boards driven into the ground in fairly shallow water, can produce excellent results, also. Many of the Game and Fish Departments across the country have details on how to construct these, and they are yours for the asking. As with any wooden structure you choose to place in the water, you'll have to refurbish the construction every couple of years.

Jigs

The technique for fishing a jig normally is exactly as the name implies, you "jig" or twitch the small lure as your retrieve it. Unfortunately, there is no iron-clad rule for the amount of action you must impart to the jig. Crappie change their minds about such things almost daily. You will find a darting, dancing retrieve is deadly one day, and the next day they prefer a painfully slow retrieve with little action. Sometimes you must hold the jig motionless next to the structure with only your slight, unavoidable hand motion furnishing all the action.

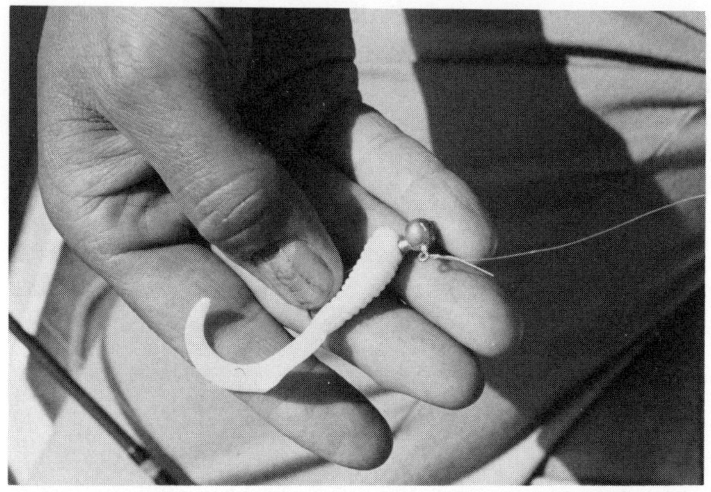

Worked at different speeds and depths until you find what they prefer, jigs can generate fantastic results. (Photo courtesy TWRA)

There is absolutely no question jigs are deadly crappie producers. You simply have to experiment a bit in discovering how they want it presented to them. No matter what method you try for crappie, *depth* is a critical factor in your success. Using jigs, the speed of your retrieve is also of keen importance.

Generally speaking, jigs work best if you twitch them with the rod tip as you retrieve. The jig dances, sinks or flutters as you work it, or "breathes" in the water. This action is intended to imitate a wounded minnow or insect, or one fearful for its life in a bad neighborhood. Both characteristics trigger strikes from crappie.

Jigging with a fly rod. Fly rods make excellent tools for use with jigs in catching crappie. You can use them either for vertical jigging, or for "flipping" a jig under and around cover. Depth control is far easier using this technique than it is while casting in the conventional manner.

Release enough line from the reel (many crappie fishermen attach small spinning reels to their fly rods for this procedure) so you can pull the jig down to the rod butt. If you're using a nine-foot fly rod, obviously you now have nine feet of line out. Another tug on the line from the reel to the second eye on the rod may release an additional two or three feet of line, etc. You quickly, easily and consistently position your jig at the correct depth for action once you find it. When you find the productive zone beneath the surface, you can stay with it every time, and don't have to worry about "counting down" the jig as it sinks.

The fly rod/jig combo can be used to work structure near the boat in a vertical manner, or used to reach stumps and brush in hard-to-hit spots where casting would require precise skill. "Flipping" the jig around visible structure with the long rod allows you to cover great amounts of water effectively as you paddle or motor quietly along. Cane poles or those of the telescoping fiberglass variety work quite well in this manner, also. They will need a linekeeper or small spinning reel taped to them, however.

Spincasting jigs. Typical gear for fishing jigs is the ultra-light outfit spooled with light line. The angler casts his offering at visible structure, or across open water and waits for it to sink to the structure below. He has an almost infinite variety of combinations available regarding depth and speed with which to work his jig. It's up to the fisherman to *experiment* until he finds the magic combo of depth and speed. Once he does so, the

Jigs and ultra-light tackle combine to make crappie fishing more fun and effective.

ice chest starts gaining weight.

It seems a common mistake often made comes from using jigs which are too large, and/or reeling in overly fast. When fishing deeper water, you often feel the need for heavier jigs because nobody likes to sit there all day waiting for a 1/64 oz. jig to sink 20 feet in the water. The same type inclination comes out on windy days when casting the tiny baits in any direction other than downwind is rather impossible. Solve both situations by attaching a couple of BB-size split shot to your line some 18 or 24 inches above the jig. The weight of the split shot will solve the problem, and positioned well above the jig, the little weights have practically no affect on the action of the lure.

When working shallow-water structure, you will find the use of a small bobber is truly helpful for spincasting jigs. Pick the smallest one you can see from a distance, perhaps no larger than one inch in size. Brightly colored floats are more easily missed when crappie sink them, too. Casting the jig and float to shallow structure allows you to control the depth the jig works. It also allows you to impart a number of antics to the mini fishfoolers. You can reel very slowly and steadily if the fish seem to like that number, or you can twitch and slide the float back to the boat. Another excellent way to work the jig and float combo is with a start-stop action. Each time you stop retrieving the rig, the jig falls downward in the water. Crappie have a thing about falling jigs, and you'll probably get the majority of your hits when the jig is sinking. Set the hook gently at the first wobble of the float. It doesn't take a crappie long to figure out lead and plastic are hard to digest; he'll spit the jig out rather quickly.

Incidentally, small jigs require small diameter line. The heavy stuff is not flexible enough to allow the smaller jigs to work the way their designers envisioned. Also, unless you're trolling a jig, you should check it often to insure the jig hangs correctly on the line. Hold the line in your fingers and look at how the jig hangs in mid-air. Properly tied, the jig should hang horizontally. If it doesn't, slide the knot forward or back on the hook eye until it does, or retie the knot. The jig needs to be balanced on the line to provide the correct action. (When trolling jigs, the lure is usually attached with a small loop knot.)

When fishing with light line, check it *regularly* for nicks and abrasions. I don't know how they do

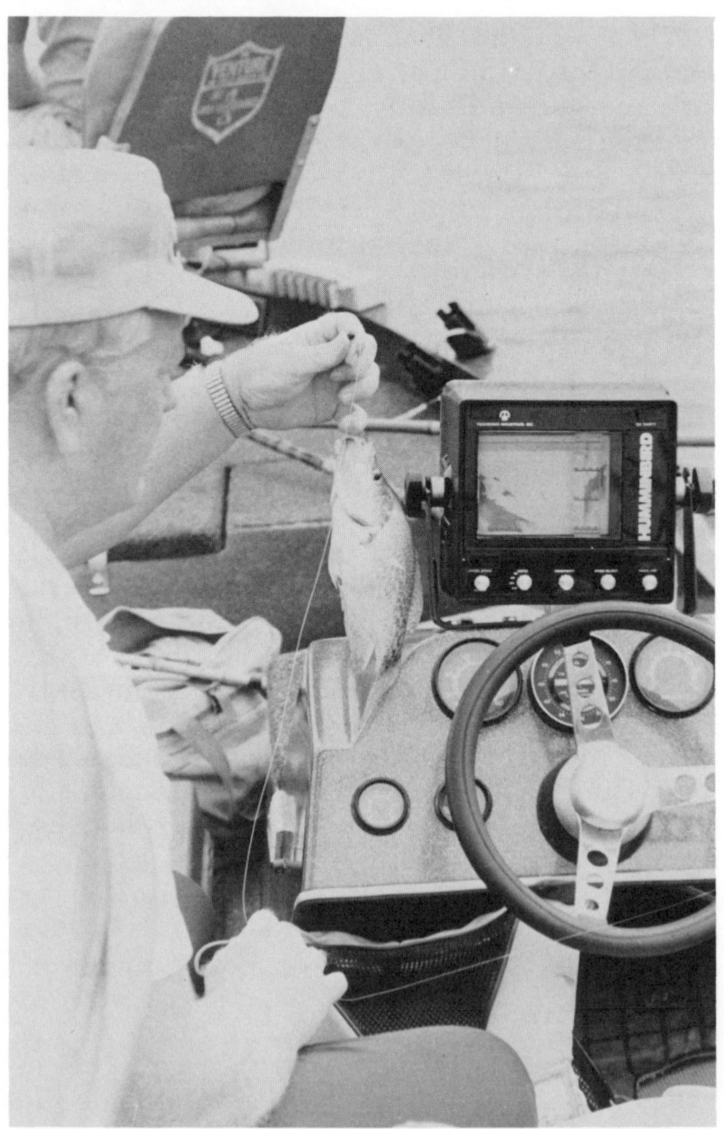

Learn the basics of reading your depthfinder, and crappie fishing success can become almost routine. (Photo courtesy John Phillips)

it, but the really big slab crappie have a way of waiting until after you get a weak spot in your four-pound string before loading on your jig.

To summarize, jig fishing is an excellent way to fill your ice chest with crappie. Many anglers swear jigs are more productive than live minnows, and limit their attempts to the little artificial devils regardless of other available methods. If you're new at the game, remember the importance of a limber rod tip, as the stiff ones make it tough to set the hook without ripping through the crappie's paper-like mouth. Whether you select a flyrod/spinning reel combo, or go the conventional route with spincasting tackle, it becomes keenly important that you *experiment* with depth and speed of retrieve in order to find the crappie's preference for the day. *Work all the water* before moving to a new location. When you find what they want, hammer your efforts at that depth and speed. Move when the action slows, and return to the same place later, as crappie often move back onto the same structure shortly after you leave it.

The size line you use is a trade-off many times. The two, four and six-pound mono is great for tiny jigs, providing the best action from the lure. The thin mono doesn't perform well in the presence of snags, however. Fishing brushy areas usually demands you switch to heavier line unless you happen to own a tackle store.

Finally, remember depth control is more important than the color jig you use.

Trolling

I've heard many knowledgeable crappie fishermen say these fish are not hard to catch, they're just hard to *find*. There's a lot of truth to that statement.

Trolling allows you to cover a great deal of water in your search for crappie. Those who master this technique often return to the dock with a healthy number of fish when others do not. Occasionally, you'll find a crappie fisherman whose only method for catching fish is trolling, and he'll probably be quick to tell you all the other techniques are a waste of time. I disagree with that, but will quickly admit trolling is a fine way to capture tablefare.

If you're reasonably skilled at reading a depth-finder, you can work your boat along drop-offs and/or weed lines slightly offshore, following the structure as it meanders back and forth. A few rod holders clamped or mounted on your boat will allow you to literally "sweep" the area at a variety of depths as you motor along quietly with your trolling motor. Minnows, jigs, small artificial lures, or a combination of all three can be employed as you troll. Give the fish a choice, and see what they select on the menu.

When rigging your offerings for trolling, there are many ways to produce the pay-off. Initially, you may be wise to present the best variety of action and depth you can generate for the fish. No point trolling over an area where the fish have their taste buds set for the one thing you didn't offer.

Almost "anything goes" when you're trolling

Slow trolling with two or more baits in the water is an excellent technique. (Photo courtesy TWRA)

for crappie. The objective is to find the area, the depth, and the action the fish want at any given time of day or night. You basically use your imagination to figure out how many different ways you can present bait to the fish, based upon the contents of your tackle box. For example:

One rod holder clamped to the side of your boat can be fitted with a spinning rod sporting four-pound line and a 1/32 oz. maribou jig. As that rod is positioned horizontally to the water surface, another is positioned on the same side of the boat at a 45-degree angle to the surface. The second one sports a lead weight on the end of the line (snagless bell sinker type) and a pair of plastic grubs on trailer lines of different lengths. On the opposite side of the boat, a third rod holder may secure your old flyrod onto which is trolled a tiny flasher blade or propeller above a gold hook holding a lively minnow. (Hook the minnow through the mouth or eye sockets, otherwise he will turn sideways and spin as he moves thru the water.) Your final presentation can be on the fourth rod which trolls a small artificial lure, either a mini crankbait or a delicious-looking tidbit of plastic with a spinner blade twirling ahead or above it. If you *really* want to "rake" the water for fish, you can tie multiple drop lines and trailers to each of the rigs, driving the fish nuts with so many goodies to choose from as you pass overhead.

It is possible the Game and Fish boys could frown upon this sort of thing in selected states, so you better check the laws. I personally don't know of anyplace it is illegal, but that won't keep you out of jail when the warden calls it to your attention.

Regarding specifics, jigs are best tied to your line with a small loop knot, the knot not to exceed the length of the jig. Begin by trolling at the slowest speed possible, increasing the speed very gradually during subsequent passes over the area you feel should produce.

When a fish takes one of your baits, let the motion of the boat do the hook-setting. Wait until the rod has a definite bend in it, indicating there is a fish on the other end. Then merely remove the rod from the holder and reel the little sweetheart into the boat. Don't stop the trolling motor. Chances are, before you get Number One into captivity, one or more of the other rods will need attention from the school you found. Once you find the pattern for depth, speed and bait the fish want, you can pitch a few marker buoys out to the side for reference and either continue trolling back and forth, or anchor and work the area by casting or still fishing. When you wear that bunch out, crank up the road show and go find another school.

Variety in your offerings, *variety* in the depth by using different weights and line sizes, and *variety* in boat speed until you hit it right, will make this technique work on every day of the week whose name ends in the letter "Y."

Like any other method for catching crappie, trolling is not an automatic guarantee for success, although it is truly an excellent producer. Trolling is more effective when used in fairly shallow lakes or portions of rivers and creeks. It can be tough to produce stringers by trolling when the fish are holding in deep water, as your ability to control depth and action are limited the further your bait gets from your fingertips. While I'm

"Slabs" like these often spawn in deeper water. (Photo courtesy Bob Dennie)

hesitant to suggest lures and jigs have a mind of their own, my experience with them in deep water is similar to ones you may have had the first time you left a puppy in the house alone all day thinking he was housebroken. More times than not, you're idea of what's happening doesn't prove to be exactly correct.

Night Fishing

Primarily a hot-weather pursuit, fishing for crappie after dark can produce stringers of fish worthy of wakening your best friend at 2:00 o'clock in the morning for some heavy-duty bragging. Regardless of his initial comments. He or she may not be thrilled over your late-hour knocking at the door; maybe not even speak to you for the next 48 hours afterwards. But within three or four days, you can bet your family jewels that person will come around asking questions about "how, when and where!"

During July and August when the temperatures are bouncing the mercury around the top of the thermometer, days spent on the lake or river can result in little more than sunburn and excessive beer drinking. (There are some excellent techniques for catching crappie at those times, too, as will be explained later!) Taking a break from the parching summer heat and general inactivity for fishermen during the day can be accomplished with minimum effort and equipment. If you haven't tried night fishing for crappie, you're ready for a genuine treat. It's fun. And very productive.

After-dark temperatures are welcome relief

Stumps located on slopes and drop-offs will hold crappie in spring and fall.

from the blistering summer days. Cool, refreshing breezes greet the nighttime angler, and the absence of obnoxious water skiers is a reward in itself.

You need a high-intensity light to attract insects. The insects try to kiss the light and fall into the water. When they do, minnows and small fish gather around to feed on the bugs. Once the minnows are actively feeding, the crappie appear on the scene like magic. So do white bass (stripes), largemouth, bream, catfish and a number of other species ready to take advantage of the free lunch.

A variety of floating night lights are marketed for your convenience. You can accomplish the same results with a lantern designed for camping adventures. You will need an oversize shade or top for the lantern, extending well beyond the diameter of the glass cylinder surrounding the burning mantle. This reflects more light into the water. Hang the lantern on a cane pole or a store-bought bracket attached to the boat. Position the light source as close to the water surface as you can without getting it wet. To protect your eyes from the blinding glare of the lantern, I suggest you fashion a reflector from tinfoil, placing it on the backside of the globe nearest to the boat. This intensifies the light going into the water, and allows you to see rod tips, bobbers in the water, and other essentials like the coffee cup in the boat.

If you don't have a lantern, you can hollow out a piece of foam and position a sealed-beam car headlight in it. Run the wire to an extra battery in the boat and you're in business. You can position the light in the water with a pole to keep the thing where you want it, or just toss it overboard to float. So long as the wires on the topside of the headlight don't get wet, the sealed-beam will work, whether touching the water or not. I reccommend you don't get the glass hot before dunking it in the water, but once it's there, water won't hurt it.

Before you drop anchor on the lake or river to harvest a bunch of nocturnal crappie, you should calculate where the fish are likely to be located. In the summertime, you can count on crappie living close to deep water. Use a topo map, or your own knowledge of the lake, to find a long, sloping point going away from shore and featuring a drop-off into the deep liquid on the end or side(s). If there happens to be a crop of brush or stumps on the point, that's a real bonus.

Check out the topo map to find the junction of two creeks or rivers as they come into or down the

Finding and fishing the open-water drop-offs is a sure way to enjoy action with crappie. (Photo courtesy Santee Cooper Country)

lake. Where these two channels intersect can be an absolute "honey hole" for night fishing. Crappie following either or both migration routes will meet and set up summer housekeeping at that junction. Position your boat on top of the drop-off for either channel. Anchoring back a few yards on the flat may provide zilch in the way of fillets. Sometimes crappie will take a tour for a few yards to check out the lights, and sometimes you must spread the picnic blanket virtually in their living room to get attention. In the summertime, they live *on* the drop-off, not over the top of it somewhere on the flat shoulder.

Underwater islands and humps or ridges are

excellent places to stake your claim for night fishing. If you have caught crappie at those places before, so much the better. And if you have been paying attention, you may well have sunk a man-made brush pile there a few months beforehand. If that's the case, you might even get a two a.m. smile from your mother-in-law when you show her the results!

State, Federal and County employees all love the fun and challenge of building bridges over water. This not only gives them something to do, but also creates a mecca for night fishermen. You don't even need a boat. Crappie have a fondness for bridge pilings and rip-rap. The most practical way to hoist fillets from the water around bridges is to stand on the bridge itself and lower your light source into effective range of the water below. You'll need to position the lantern within about a foot of the water surface. (Other types of illumination are impractical unless you wish to carry a heavy battery and 75 pounds of lamp wire from the parking lot.)

Attach some five or six feet of lightweight chain or heavy wire to the handle of the lantern before tying on the rope. Then you can lower the ignited lantern down from the bridge safely. Burning lanterns make an awful noise when they splash into the water. The chain or wire prevents the heat of the lantern from burning thru the rope you tie to the bridge railing. Attracting crappie at night around bridges is easy. Losing burning lanterns into the depths is expensive.

Some of the most memorable nights I have had fishing for crappie took place on boat docks constructed by people living on the lakeshore. One particular stretch of real estate purchased for a homesite was located on shore near a sharp drop-off into deeper water of the lake. The owners had the foresight to install an automatic timer on the lights at the end of the dock, and the kindness to allow me to construct a few artificial housing projects within fishing distance. There was hardly a night of the summer when we could not sit on the dock in comfort, drinking our ice tea and pulling in crappie, bream and catfish at will.

When night fishing, you normally use minnows for bait. If you're anchored on a point or at the junction of two creek channels, you have to rely on the power of your light source to draw your tablefare. Once the smaller fish begin swimming under the light, you'll be in business. Flourescent line makes it easier to see the action when a fish smacks your bait, and having several baited poles in the water at different depths will make it easier to discover the optimum zone for the fun. Having an ultralight rod and reel in the boat rigged with a small jig is great insurance. When the action hits a flurry of success, tossing the little jig into the water can speed up the results because you don't have to stop frequently to impale a new minnow on your hook. It's a good idea to have a rod or two on standby when night fishing, rigged with small jigs and ready for use. They can be highly productive when the crappie move into the light and the time spent rebaiting could be better spent hauling fish aboard.

Your night light usually draws small shad minnows, and they swim in thick schools just below the surface. You can tie a series of loops in your line, thread 1/0 or 2/0 hooks onto the loops and tie

Night fishing under the lanterns is one way to beat the heat and bring in braggin' stringers of crappie. (Photo courtesy John Phillips)

a lead weight to the end of the line. Drop this rig into the school of minnows; snatch it upwards to snag one or more shad. Then either remove the little fish for use on your other poles, or merely lower the snatch rig back into the water just below the school of minnows where the crappie are feeding. Presto! A baited hook of natural food for which you never had to pay the bait shop owner.

A final word on night fishing. Even during the hottest period of summer when night fishing is best, you will need a light jacket for comfort when the sun disappears. Something about the moisture and cooling effect of being on the water at night makes this true. Hot coffee, a talkative companion, and a warm jacket will make the night go better while you wait on your light to do its thing with the fish.

This technique will not work year-round, but during the summer months, it will produce crappie in greater numbers than you care to clean in the wee hours of the morning.

Driftfishing

Done properly, this can be one of the most effective techniques going for catching quantities of crappie. There's more to it than turning off the engine, dropping over a baited hook and propping your feet up on the gunnel while the wind pushes the boat around. A lot more!

Driftfishing is a procedure for taking good numbers of fish, but you still must apply the technique in productive territory. It will work year-round, but only when you are working the right depths and in the general portion of the lake or river where crappie are holding.

Basically, driftfishing requires multiple poles be positioned in rod holders all around the bow of the boat. Some anglers construct a wooden shelf-like apparatus which spans the bow area of the boat from gunnel to gunnel. To this shelf (usually a 2 x 6 board) are attached five or six rod holders, angled out at different positions to form a fan or "spider leg" pattern.

Your depthfinder must be positioned in easy view for reading, and the trolling motor is generally bolted to the side of the boat by your seat instead of up in the bow. The sonar transducer is attached to the foot of the trolling motor.

All of the poles are equipped with dual-hook rigs, similar to those used in tightlining; ie: two hooks 18 inches apart with a lead weight on the bottom end.

Motor to the area where fish are holding in that particular season, find the drop-offs and mark them with floating bouys. You should mark off a long stretch of the drop if possible, then work along from one bouy to the next.

Once you have located and marked your intended path of travel, you break out the poles and get set up. Adjust the amount of line let out on each pole to provide a wide variety initially. Put one almost on bottom, the next two feet above bottom, the next four feet above, etc. In this manner you can offer a minnow at *many* depths as you move. If you have out six poles, you can offer your bait at 12 different depths!

Use the trolling motor only to keep the boat on target along the edge of the drop-off. And use it sparingly; a brief kick of the prop now and then to keep the boat positioned is enough. Work your way very slowly along the marked route. When

Black crappie like these prefer clear, less polluted waters. (Photo courtesy Bob Dennie)

you find action, note the depth of the productive bait. If another fish or two dines on a minnow at the same general depth, you may then adjust all your poles to position bait at that depth.

Underwater, the approaching bunch of minnows looks to a crappie like a whole school of snacks moving by. Positioned at the right depth after you found it, this multiple offering is deadly. You litterally "sweep" the water in a wide swath as you move along slowly. As always when crappie fishing, you must be observant to insure success. When a fish is hooked, check out the depthfinder reading to *see what depth water* you are in. The hook upon which the fish is caught will tell you how deep the crappie are, but not whether the fish are near bottom or suspended. This can save you a material amount of time if you find it necessary to change your route of travel. When you see a pattern, you may wish to alter the boat's route slightly in or out from the bouys, covering either deeper or more shallow bottom depths.

It all may sound rather easy, but driftfishing done in this manner definitely is not the easiest technique for capturing fillets. One of the more effective ones, yes. Easy? No.

By virtue of having multiple poles in the water, you are going to encounter multiple hang-ups on snags. Eventually, you're going to have a bass or pike chomp your minnow and get all the poles tangled when he makes a run. And you're going to drift through a school of hungry crappie and have several of them take your baits at the same time, causing mass confusion (and laughter) as fish come sailing in over the sides all at once and get everything in the boat tangled together in a wad!

You may find effective driftfishing requires a partner in the boat to share in the fun. And in controlling the lines. When you encounter an aggressive snag below, remember to "jiggle" the rig free. *Don't snatch it* or you'll be there forever with six poles to contend with!

Miscellaneous

You have seen some methods here which work for catching fish regularly under a variety of situations. Crappie are easy to catch, and happily, take a lure or minnow presented to them almost any way you can think of, providing the depth and speed are to their liking. Here are a few more ideas you may want to try.

Cane poles. Most of us probably started crappie fishing with one of these, so I'm sure you're familiar with the standard routine of standing on the bank dunking minnows in treetops during the springtime spawning runs. However, you may not have tried doing the same thing using jigs instead of minnows, and it works quite well. In slightly deeper water, or perhaps an area with standing timber, a jig tied to the line of your cane pole can be worked effectively to place the lure smack on the bark of the tree or stump. Simply raise the pole up and down slowly, keeping the jig within an inch of the tree. The added "reach" of a long pole under these circumstances makes quite a difference in not spooking the fish.

Poles rigged with either single or multiple jigs can be excellent fish-finders, too. Lower the jig(s) into the water to a chosen depth and hold them there. Your natural hand movement usually will

Wholesome outdoor fun for the family; that's what crappie fishing is all about!

provide sufficient action for the jig to generate a strike. If nothing happens within about 30 seconds, change depths by lowering or raising the pole, and repeat the process. When you find the correct depth for the fish, you can switch to a cork float, or continue tight-lining there.

Fly fishing. When the willow flies hatch in summer, fish of all species seem to be drawn to the fracus along shore. The crappie are no different. They'll come to shore and gorge themselves on the abundant food source. A small, floating fly vaguely resembling a May fly adult will fool enough of them to make you strain trying to lift the stringer. Flick the dry fly near shore where the real ones are dropping into the water, or use a roll cast to get your fly under overhanging tree limbs. When the crappie takes it, resist the urge to set the hook hard, remembering the tender mouth they have. You'll catch a large variety of fish in this manner, bream, bass, etc.

Trailer lines on plugs. A two-foot trailer of six-pound mono attached to a small spinner can double your fun. Attach a plastic grub or curly-tail jig to the trailer, and you'll present a double whammy for the crappie to consider. Some will take the spinner, others will prefer the smaller jig. The spinner keeps the jig submerged, and the blade action it has telegraphs down the line to make the jig dance like crazy. Cast this outfit into shore and around structure in early summer or fall, and you should be pleasantly surprised with the results.

Depthfinders

I saved this subject for last, as depthfinders are a pet topic of mine. I have written a full-blown,

This ice chest is fast getting filled as these anglers hit it right on July crappie.

fully-illustrated book on how to use the things, and some of you may have read it. (If not, there just *happens* to be ordering information in the rear of this book!) Depthfinders are to successful year-round crappie fishing what flour is to hot biscuits.

Crappie are very structure-oriented, remaining in approximate contact with it almost at all times. Granted, crappie frequently suspend off bottom, but *they do it in relation to the structure below.* They'll suspend over the drop-off, over the creek beds, or along the weed lines. I've never found these fish suspended over a barren, featureless underwater flat. Sometimes they may feed up and over a river bed shoulder onto such a flat if their prey goes that way, but they don't stay there long. And they sure don't take up residence there.

Whether you use a flasher or graph depthfinder, its value to you comes via providing information on the structure below. Generally, if you know where to fish during each month of the year, all you must do is find the appropriate structure in the correct depth water, and you find the crappie. You don't have to be an expert on sonar to find the old river bed in the middle of the lake during hot summer months. When you do, however, you'll find crappie there. In early spring, before the spawn, the depthfinder can guide you to the underwater islands, humps and ridges near the mouths of bays and large creeks entering the lake. That's where the crappie will be holding. And when you're faced with catching crappie suspended off shore somewhere, the depthfinder allows you to motor along the edge of whatever type structure you encounter, never straying far from potentially productive water until you locate the fish.

If you're following a weedline edge, for example, watch the bottom reading on your unit carefully. You'll see it fluctuate from a bright (or dark, in the case of graphs) readout when you are over hard ground, to a softer, less distinct readout when you pass over the vegetation. If you turn up the sensitivity on your unit until you get a good second bottom reading, or "echo," you can simplify the interpretation greatly. Every time you pass over the weeds below, they are going to absorb some of the sonar signal energy being shot from your transducer. When that happens, your second bottom reading will disappear. Simple as that! You know immediately, you're over weeds again instead of on the outer edge.

Another trick with sonar which can be helpful, is learning how to spot fish holding *inside* brush or treetops. Sounds impossible, but it's not. Trees and brush accumulate various types of growth on their surfaces after long periods underwater. The wood itself starts to soften and decay, also. On the other hand, the scales of fish are hard, and will reflect a more strong returning signal to your unit than will the softer treetop. Turn *down* the sensitivity on your unit to look inside the confines of an underwater tree. The signals from the tree will fade as they are weak. Fish present there will continue to give noticably stronger returning signals! No point fishing in a treetop if there are no fish in it, right?

Depthfinders also earn their keep by telling you quickly when your lake has an oxygen turnover problem. Many lakes suffer this phenomenon at least once a year. If you're fish-hunting one fine summer afternoon and see absolutely no blips or blurbs on the dial of your sonar below a certain depth, take notice. Sonar won't tell you the oxygen content of water all by itself. But if it shows you a particular level of the lake which is totally devoid of all fish life, you can make the rather simple deduction by yourself. If you were planning to fish 20 feet down the shoulder of the old river channel, and nothing is living down past the 15-foot mark, revise your plan based on the sonar info.

Depthfinders are covered in more detail in Chapter Six. There also are some excellent examples shown of fish on and around structure at various times of the year, taken from actual graph paper readings.

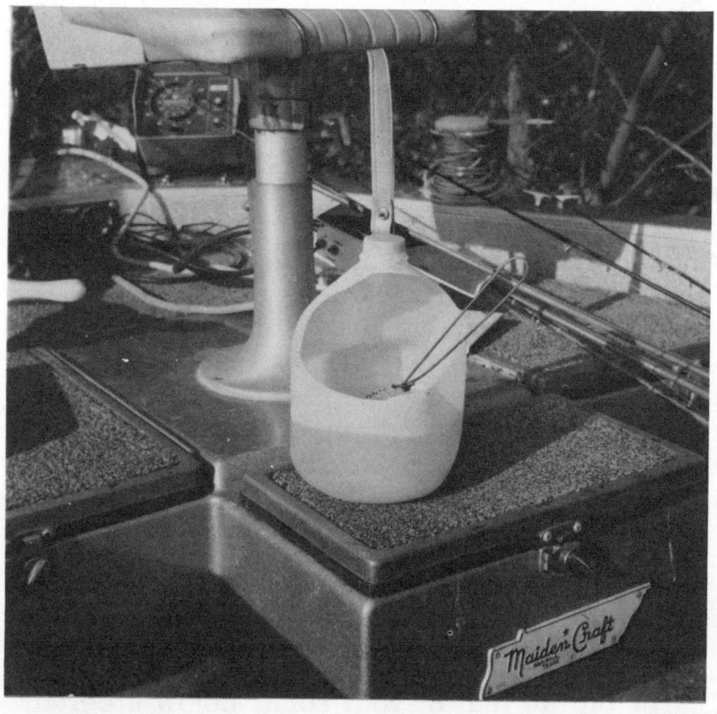

A cut-out plastic milk jug makes a fine spare minnow container.

Flyrods equipped with small spinning reels make great combos for jig fishing.

Crappie are easier, more predictable in July and August than any other time of year!

4

Crappie Anytime You Want 'Em

One of the prime problems one encounters when trying to earn a living with a rod and reel, gun, sleeping bag and typewriter, is that the game and the weather rarely cooperate with deadlines set by magazine editors. Everything would be fine if the editors weren't so picky. They always insist on facts and photos for proof. You either succeed in catching fish or shooting game, or you don't sell the article. I never sold an article on how bad the wind was blowing for four days, or one dealing with the effect of planning an entire hunting trip around the expertise of a professional guide in Colorado who stayed drunk the whole time I was there.

There are two kinds of outdoor writers: those who are paid regularly for being on the staff of a magazine, and those who freelance material to whomever they can get to buy it. The staffers get their expenses paid for them, plus receive money for writing the article. The freelancers pay their own way and occasionally sell enough words about the adventure to break even. Unfortunately, I fell into the latter class, as all the major outdoor magazines already had a full compliment of staffers by the time I learned to type.

Successful freelancers are required to be sneaky in order to survive. The unreasonable burden of having to produce actual photos of your success makes it necessary to use whatever devious methods at your disposal in order to capture your intended quarry. Short of resorting to dynamite or some other method which may have been frowned upon by the authorities, I probably used every trick in the book to insure results. One of my pet goals was to secure "insurance material" in advance. This meant having three or four fish in the cooler *before* meeting the "expert" I was supposed to interview, etc. Amazing how much better the day goes if you can take the pictures quickly before you find out all the conditions are wrong.

I rationalized away this basic flaw in character by admitting my fondness for eating regularly on the money earned by selling the articles. However, getting "insurance material" before the trip began was often no small chore. Fortunately, if I couldn't come up with bass, sauger or whatever we needed, I could almost always count on hauling in a few good crappie. Sometimes, the editor was more interested in the name recognition factor of my celebrity or expert than he was in the species of fish we caught. Either way, I managed to salvage many trips by having crappie on hand for photos. This is one reason why I'm convinced the info in this book will work for you. I had to catch crappie under a wide variety of conditions, on a number of lakes which were new to me, and in practically every month of the year for many years.

Overcast days often produce the best action. (Photo courtesy Santee Cooper Country)

Basically, to catch these fish consistently year-round, you must understand where they move to during the four major seasons. The various techniques previously discussed will work extremely well under most circumstances, if applied in the general area where the fish are living at the time. There is a summary of crappie movements and migrations to be found at the end of this chapter. Dates are based mainly on how the fish respond to changes in water temperatures, and those shown are taken from the state of Kentucky as it is fairly centrally located in the States. You may have to alter the dates a bit to match the appropriate temperatures and seasons for your area.

Your depthfinder is a critical piece of equipment in your successful attempts to catch crappie. With one notable exception while fishing for giant bream in Africa, I can not remember a time when the advantages available from sonar would not have increased the catch. And that particular experience was on Lake Kariba in Zimbabwe where the water is very clear. The big bream (up to six pounds) concentrate in the weed beds which spot an otherwise barren bottom in water seven to twelve feet deep. One simply motors slowly along until he sees a weed bed, then positions the boat over a hole in the vegetation and drops his bait to the bottom. Had the water not been so clear, it would have been extremely difficult to find the weedbeds without sonar, however.

My friend, Lanny Deal, is a guide of fine reputation who fishes on Lake Eufaula in Alabama. Lanny has refined his use of depthfinders for catching crappie into a fine art, and does so handily virtually any day of the year. Either using a topo map or his knowledge of the lake, Lanny looks for a deep creek channel with sharply-defined ledges, and prefers a decided drop from seven or eight feet down to 20 or 30, deeper if possible. The key factor is that the drop is sharp and not a gentle one in angle.

He idles his boat along the drop-off in water 15

to 25 feet, looking for flashes on his sonar in the 10 to 20-foot range. In Lake Eufaula, these drop-offs usually have underwater standing timber. Each time he finds something generating multiple signals in the desired area, he drops over a floating marker bouy. After putting out several bouys, he switches over to his graph unit and goes back over the spots again, noting which readings were from trees, from fish, and trees with fish, too. The graph tells him exactly how deep the fish are holding, and once he has verified the "where and how deep" information, he's ready for the fun.

Lanny doesn't anchor the boat by his marked spot. Instead, he uses his trolling motor and eases around the appropriate bouys. He has a third unit mounted in the bow, the transducer attached to the foot of the trolling motor. As his sonar has disclosed the correct depth where the fish are holding, Lanny sets his cane poles to that depth and he's ready. Depending upon which unit he takes the fish's depth from, he adjusts the poles to compensate for the distance the transducer is beneath the water surface. For example, if you read fish at 12 feet on a transducer mounted to the foot of your trolling motor, set your bait to ride at about 13 feet deep. This is because the transducer is probably a foot beneath the surface when it gives you the reading. Crappie are notorious for being horizontal feeders, rarely coming up or going down more than a few inches to take a bait.

Lanny keeps spare bouys in the bow, and when fish are caught while moving around, drops another on the spot immediately. (Actually, he drops it about ten feet past the spot to prevent get-

Fun for the whole family, crappie fishing provides outdoor recreation plus great meals at home. (Photo courtesy Bob Dennie)

ting tangled.) Wind permitting, this method works well on river ledges in the main lake sporting similar drops. If he finds fish holding too deep for using the cane poles, Lanny switches to open-face spinning gear with 12-pound line. By knowing the exact length of the rod, he can present his bait correctly by pulling line from the tip to the base three, four or more times until the proper amount of line is out. Care must be taken to allow for the distance you will hold the rod tip above the water surface with this method. Using light wire hooks and a couple of split shot, Lanny moves slowly to allow the line to hang vertically below without a float.

Like many expert crappie fishermen, Lanny doesn't set the hook; he merely lifts the pole or rod, or begins reeling in the line. Tender mouths on the fish make hook-setting unnecessary and often a hard-snatched hook will tear out. A landing net is used also for the same reason.

Fishing regularly, Lanny can follow the fish as they move from the deeper parts of the lake into more shallow water for spawning, and then back into the channels and river ledges.

Fishing the Rivers and Creeks

I've had the pleasure of fishing for crappie with a number of genuine experts. Many come to mind, but interviews and adventures with two stand out, as they cover both general types of water you are likely to encounter. Steve McCadams is a master at boating dandy stringers of crappie from rivers and creeks; Carl Hamilton is known far and wide for his ability to catch consistent braggin' stringers in large impoundments. Here is the gist of an article I did on both of them and their techniques:

Steve McCadams is a professional fisherman who specializes in guiding his clients on successful days filled with the fun of hauling in large numbers of good crappie. The waters he fishes around his home base at Buchanan Resort near Paris, Tennessee, are primarily rivers and creeks. Buchanan's is located on Eagle Creek where the Big Sandy and Tennessee Rivers meet. The area offers a large variety of water for fishing, sporting flats, drop-offs, bars, points, and channels. Some areas have current; some don't. Steve explains his techniques for success in these type waters as follows:

"The White Crappie, *Pomoxis annularis,* can be caught all year in open water. Most people just fish for him in the spring, ignoring the good cataches available during the rest of the year."

"Fishing during the spawning season is pretty routine, and I suppose everyone knows about fishing the buck bushes at the edge of shore at that time. When I take clients out in the spring, we usually work with poles that have only three or four feet of line on them, using a float and dropping a minnow straight down into small openings in the brush. We use a couple of large split shot above the hook, and fish 12 to 18-inches deep. A normal day will produce 50 or more crappie, many in the two-pound class which we call "slabs.""

"The main reason I take my clients to the shoreline for spawning season fishing is because it's easier for *them* to fish that way. We certainly could catch a very fine stringer of crappie out in

Using your depthfinder to locate underwater structure in the appropriate part of the lake or river will allow you to catch crappie year-round.

the open water on those same days. Crappie don't all head for the banks to spawn at the same time. If you master the open-water fishing methods, you can do well with that technique all the time, even when everyone else is working the banks."

Tight-line fishing - "bottom bumping" with no cork - is the bread-and-butter method Steve uses to get fish for his clients during the rest of the year. Remember, he is fishing an area where a large number of bottom configurations come together; the mouth of the Big Sandy River has over 90 underwater drop-offs beneath its placid surface!

The equipment Steve uses for open water fishing consists of a ten-foot telescopic fiberglass pole, to which is taped a linekeeper filled with 40-pound monofilament. In addition to being extremely sensitive, the little, lightweight pole won't tire your arm and wrist after several hours of fishing. The business end of the rig is made with 25-pound mono and attached to the main line with a snap swivel. A two-ounce bell sinker is attached to the end of the terminal rig to hold down the pair of 4/0 wire hooks.

"These local waters are a bit on the cloudy side (giving fairly low visibility due to suspended particles in the water) so I can use the heavier line for the leader rig," Steve explains. "If your area features more clear liquid, you may wish to drop down to perhaps 12-pound mono. In clearer water, the smaller line would probably work better."

"A depthfinder is necessary to find the desired structure. Use a trolling motor, keep your bow into the wind, if any, and work along over the drop-offs, river beds, tree-tops, etc. Bump the bottom with the lead sinker as you move slowly across the area. When you feel the sinker strike a stump or some other underwater cover, hold the pair of minnows motionless right next to the stump for a few moments. If he doesn't take it then, work your bait slowly and completely around the piece of structure."

"You will get your rig hung up frequently with this method. It's only natural. But when you do, resist the urge to jerk the line because all that will accomplish is to lodge the hook(s) firmly into the underwater object. Instead, just ease your pole up and down gently to "jiggle" your hook free of the snag. The bell sinker on the bottom of your rig aids to free the hook on the downward motion. If you're really hung badly and cannot get free by lifting and dropping the sinker, the heavy mono allows you to pull free as a last resort by straightening the thin wire hook. Even so, it's a good idea to have several spare rigs tied up in advance. If you do lose your rig by breaking off, you can be back in business in only seconds with a single, quick knot!"

Employing the open-water methods which Steve uses so effectively on crappie, you will catch a variety of other species, too, including bass, catfish, sauger and large bream. This increases both fun and the weight of your stringer. With practice, you will develop a keen sensitivity to the "feel" of that sinker bouncing bottom and sending signals back thru the light pole. Pretty soon you can tell whether you are fishing a mud bottom or on hard gravel, striking a stump or brushing a tree top. Steve says your hands become your eyes when you're tight-lining!

Floating structure markers are quite useful

Early-morning crappie taken from shallow-water structure by casting jigs and retrieving slowly.

when working bars and points underwater. The markers help you lay out the drop-off below by tossing one overboard every now and then as you work the slope the first time. The second and third pass along the drop-off can be done with ease then by simply following the highway of markers. Floating markers are good for pinpointing a particularly good stump, also. If two or three fish were taken from a single spot on the first pass, drop a marker and come back to it in a few minutes.

When you locate a good spot for crappie in the open water, remember that finding it again the

following weekend may be plenty tough unless you mark it somehow. Line up bouys, points, tree snags on shore, etc. into a triangle centered at your location. In this manner you can return to the spot easily later on—without spending time searching again.

"The purpose in having two hooks on this rig is to allow the fisherman to present his bait at different depths," Steve says. "The double hooks are not an attempt to catch two crappie at the same time, although this happens quite often. Normally, you will catch more crappie on one hook than the other, even though they are only some 18 inches apart in the water."

Crappie frequently are suspended a few feet off bottom, even though the cover could be laying beneath them. Catching fish consistantly on the top hook will tell you this is true on a given day.

Another thing to remember is that a crappie seldom moves far up or down in depth to go after a minnow. It's easy to miss the good fishing because your bait is too deep. You have to find cover in order to find crappie, but this doesn't mean the fish will always be concentrated at the base of the structure.

"If you aren't fishing around cover—and getting hung in it once and a while—you're wasting time trying for crappie," Steve continued. "I immediately go for cover where there is a drop-off and/or shelf in the bottom. Most of the time the fish will be along the slope of the drop-off, between the two extremes of the contour, and this is where you should begin fishing. Keep in mind that they may run up on top of the bar to feed sometimes and then return to the edge. Occasionally they will work off the deep side, too. You may have to try all the possibilities before hitting fish, but as a general rule, working the mid depth of a drop-off first is best."

"I have a great deal of confidence in the rise and fall of the water level as a tip-off about where to find crappie. You can bet good money that a fall in the water level, say two or three tenths of a foot a day, will cause the fish to move into a little deeper water. Conversely, a rise in water will cause them to come up a little. This is a pattern you can take advantage of, and it really works."

"A cloudy day will cause the fish to come up in depth, also. This is especially true in spring and fall fishing. Even in August when the mercury has been hitting the 100-degree mark and most other things have little effect on crappie, a cloudy day will make them come up slightly," he concludes.

Big Lakes and Impoundments

While Steve is busy filling ice chests with crappie taken from creeks and rivers, another expert I interviewed is doing the same thing on large, open waters of man-made impoundments. If this is your kind of fishing territory, listen up. Here's how it's done on big water:

Carl Hamilton is the owner of Sportsman's Lodge on Kentucky Lake, and has enjoyed the benefits of many years' experience in fishing some of America's finest crappie water. I don't know how he would do on Wall Street, but when Carl Hamilton speaks, fishermen listen! When I fished with Carl we caught an impressive stringer of crappie. And I listened.

"One of the great things about crappie fishing is that every member of the family can enjoy it—from the little tykes up to the grandparents. Crappie are a lot of fun, and they can be caught year around," Carl began, pulling in a slab-sided fish. "It's not an expensive fishing habit; there's no need for a big bass boat and a floating store full of tackle. In fact, during the spawning season, you don't even need a motor. You can paddle or let the wind drift you along. You can even fish right from the bank."

"So crappie fishing is something we can all participate in, and everyone can catch crappie. In most lakes they are abundantly available. There may be some "secret" or modified method people have developed in a particular body of water, but the key is always in finding the depth of water the crappie are using. Then all you have

Water temperatures basically determine where you will find the crappie. (Photo courtesy John Phillips)

to do is take a contour map and find similar places in the lake where there is brush or stump rows at that same depth. Crappie will be there just about every time."

"Using ultra-light tackle with a Beetle-Spin, Grub or small jig is one of the most exciting methods of catching crappie," Carl continued. "Just cast where there is brush, or along deep drop-offs. This is generally most effective during the spawning season; ie: April or May. You can work the bank tossing these little jigs into every brushpile you see, or you can anchor and jig straight down just like you were using a minnow. Ultra-light jigging is not the most common method for catching crappie on Kentucky Lake, but many people here do it with great success."

"While we're talking about fishing with small jigs, there is another little trick you can try that is quite effective," Carl added. "Put a light float on the line above the jig and throw it in near the bank. As you work it out slowly, the float keeps the jig at whatever depth you want it, and the movement makes the jig dance along below. You'll catch a lot of crappie that way—and loose a lot less jigs!"

Carl uses the Dutch Owen fiberglass poles mentioned previously. This pole is effective year-round, but especially so in winter when the crappie bite extremely easy. When the water's real cold you have to have a pole with superior sensitivity to detect a bite.

During the colder weather, small minnows are an asset because the fish are not active in their feeding then. They'll take a small minnow before taking a large one every time. Look at the native shad minnows for example. As the weather warms

Crappie fishing in flooded timber can be excellent. (Photo courtesy The Coleman Company)

up, the shad naturally grow larger. Follow that size pattern.

Carl brought in another big crappie as I practiced my jigging technique on an aggressive snag that hadn't been there a moment before. "I use 25-pound test line, tied to a snap swivel which has an arm extending away from its body to hold the dropper line out. Another advantage of having the heavier line," he said, watching me pull both hooks free with a determined heave upwards, "is that when fishing for crappie you normally catch other kinds of fish as well. A good catfish is a lot of fun on one of these little poles, but you need the heavier line to get him into the boat."

"Many people have good luck in the spring by trolling. They put out four or five poles with floats and spider-leg them around the boat. Then they use a trolling motor to ease very slowly around an area—preferably where there are stumps. This is

Whatever the time of year, knowledge of the crappie's preferred habitat and depth makes good catches possible. (Photo courtesy TWRA)

especially good after the spawn when the fish are scattered and you don't know exactly where they are. If you catch several in one spot, you simply anchor and go to work."

"Generally, crappie will bite all day long," Carl continued. "That's a big asset for this type fishing, particularly for people who don't like to get up early! However, weather changes will have a definite effect on crappie fishing. Just *before* a storm, the fish will bite vigorously; but the moment a front hits, they'll stop cold. Crappie bite well when it's raining, too. A light, steady drizzle produces excellent fishing. In man-made lakes, dropping the water level is very detrimental to crappie fishing; raising the water improves the fishing."

"You hear a lot about water color from the fishermen as they return to the dock. Dingy water, even very muddy water, will yield crappie. But you have to be very patient and work the area much more thoroughly then. Fish are unable to see very far in that kind of situation, but obviously, they are still there. Just work the bait slowly until you get it close enough for him to hit, and he'll take it. Where legal, you can use small goldfish with good success in muddy water. They are more hardy, live longer and are more easily seen by the fish. When the water is real clear, you have to fish much deeper, and the best results are usually at night."

"Night fishing is an excellent method for catching crappie," Carl explained. "You use a gas lantern hung out over the water to draw insects. As the insects gather around the light, many of them will fall into the water, drawing minnows which feed on them. The minnows, in turn, draw the crappie. It's cooler and more pleasant fishing at night, too. Many people fish from piers and bridges this way, but you can anchor off the rocky points or brush piles with your boat and have fine fishing as well. If you can, anchor along a drop-off where there will be different depths of water on each side of the boat. Once you set up shop, don't move frequently; it takes a while to draw everybody to the scene. June, July and August are the most popular months for night fishing."

"Crappie usually feed near the bottom in large lakes. But if you're not having much luck working the bottom, try coming up about four feet and you will usually find them."

"Hooking the minnow correctly depends on how you are fishing," Carl added. "If you're not moving, hook the minnow in the back because he will produce the most action for you when hooked that way. If you're using a trolling motor, or fishing in current, hook the minnow thru the lip or eyes to prevent having him double up when pulled thru the water."

Miscellaneous Tips from the Experts

The best method for fishing where the water is clear and/or shallow is accomplished by marking the stumps or brush first. Then back off 25 or 30 feet and cast a minnow on a slip-cork into the structure.

When fishing around boat docks or piers, for best results fish right next to the posts which go down into the water.

Use the variety of methods in this book and you can fill a stringer like the one trailing this man's boat! (Photo courtesy Santee Cooper Country)

There are many ways to attract crappie into a specific area. For example, constructing stake-beds and sinking brush in the water will hold fish there. One of the best ways is to tie a bale of hay—especially alfalfa—to a stump when the water is low. This produces excellent fishing for crappie when the water comes back up.

Anise seed attracts fish. Buy a small can of anise seed at your grocers', pour it into a plastic bottle which has holes punched in it, and sink the bottle near cover where you want to fish.

Many people go out when the water is low and mark stumps by attaching branches or sticks to them. If the fishing pressure is going to be heavy in that area, it's better to make notes regarding natural landmarks which can be lined up in a particular manner so as to enable you to return to the spot when the water comes back. If you are marking a number of spots the same day, it's a good idea to take notes on a small pad which can be placed in the tackle box.

The use of contour maps is very helpful in crappie fishing regardless of the season. Contour maps are particularly valuable in the absence of having predetermined places to fish that have been marked in some way.

If you can manage to stand a 12 or 15-foot cedar tree upright on the bottom, it will produce excellent fishing for you. These trees provide good cover, and your hook is more easily jigged off branches which curve upward like that. Many people use their Christmas trees for this purpose.

Other than during the spawning season, fishing for crappie is best when there is a slight wind across the water instead of a dead calm.

During willow-fly hatches you can catch many

Cedar trees (or discarded Christmas trees) make fine crappie attractors when sunk and weighted so they stand upright. (Photo courtesy Santee Cooper Country)

crappie with a feather-tailed popping bug, presented with a fly rod. In stable water, this also works well during the spawning season in shallow water.

In the hot summer months you can work a 1/8-ounce jig slowly over the bottom by tying a two-foot trailer of leader material onto a deep-running plug like a Bomber. Troll or retrieve slowly; the wobbling lure makes the jig dance enticingly as it trails behind. This is a good method when the water is down during the summer, too.

Crappie fillets cook up much better than the whole fish. In addition, keeping the fillets away from direct contact with water on the way home will result in much firmer meat. Dropped in the bottom of your ice chest, crappie fillets will absorb water and turn into mush. Score the sides of small, whole crappie with a knife before cooking.

A plastic milk carton can prevent unkind remarks from the poor chap who must sit on the opposite end of a boat having only one minnow bucket of which you are custodian. Cut out an opening large enough for your hand to enter in the top of the carton away from the handle. Scoop up a bit of lake water and the container will hold a dip-net of minnows handily, keeping them alive and happy while giving your fishing partner a bait supply of his own.

In man-made lakes, many of the old natives living in the area will be able to remember where the springs were located before the ground was flooded. If you can find someone who can locate these springs for you, you will have much better fishing near them when the weather is very hot or very cold.

Suspended Crappie

When crappie suspend in the water, it doesn't mean they are inactive and won't bite. Something in their environment makes them seek that particular level at the moment, perhaps water temperature or oxygen content.

Frequently, after spawning crappie will suspend off bottom. Most of the time this is done close to the drop-offs and/or underwater islands. Work with your depthfinder as you move out from the spawning areas near shore, looking for these drops in bottom configuration. You should spot the schools of crappie, as well as schools of baitfish. Note and remember the depth of the schools.

Set a small float on your line approximately the same distance above your jig or minnow as was the depth of the school of crappie seen on sonar. Then troll very slowly with your trolling motor thru the area. Drop over a floating marker bouy when the action begins. You can then cast jigs or use live bait on your poles; either anchor or hover in the area with the motor.

Many lakes in the country have substantial weed growth on the bottom. Crappie will suspend along the edges of these weed patches as opposed to hanging around over the middle of them, perhaps fearful of some larger predator lurking in the vegetation. You can read the "edge" of the weedline easily with your depthfinder by observing the intensity changes in the bottom reading as you pass over the weeds and out over the bare bottom. (Rocky bottom or hard sand gives sharp, multiple readings; mud or weeds absorb part of

Crappie actions are rigidly controlled by their environment. Knowing how they react to changes pays off. (Photo courtesy Kentucky Tourism)

the signal's intensity, thus showing up as wider, weaker, less distinct bottom readings.)

If trolling doesn't produce well for you in the areas you feel sure hold suspended crappie observed on the depthfinder, switch to a very small jig on light tackle. Tip the jig with a tiny minnow, a very small piece of fish, or a mini-strip of pork rind. Position your boat on the weedline, then alternate casts to cover the inside edge of the weeds, the outside edge, and the open water as much as 10 feet away from the weedline.

Watch your line carefully as the jig sinks. If it stops before having time to hit bottom, set the hook immediately. If it twitches, increases in speed of descent, anything at all other than calmly and steadily sink in the water, you have a fish taking it and should strike instantly.

When you catch suspended crappie, mark the spot with a bouy before making another cast. Sometimes these situations can be frustrating, as you practically have to put the bait into the fish's mouths for them. Being off slightly with your presentation can result in little or no action. Suspended crappie can be finicky even with regard to the speed of your jig retrieve and/or fall in the water. Experiment with size, weight and body type; also try different combinations of speed and depth as you retrieve.

Suspended crappie can be a pain in the patience when they play hard-to-catch. But you can win the game by remembering they will take your bait if and when you figure out how they prefer it handed to them at that particular moment. If you ever forgot to buy a card and present for your spouse on your wedding anniversary, you probably still remember things were a bit stiff and

Small drop-offs near shore often hold crappie in springtime immediately after a rise in water level after heavy rains.

touchy around the house for a while afterwards. You had to be on your best behaviour and do all sorts of nice little things to appease the offended party. The extra effort was the key to creating happiness again. It's the same way when fishing for suspended crappie, although most of them prefer small, lively minnows instead of flowers and candy.

Tips and Tricks for Success

- Fisheries experts have determined fish attractors work best when constructed of about six-foot height and sunk in ten-foot water. The top of the brushpile is thus four feet beneath the surface and easily fished with a variety of methods. The six-foot span of structure also will provide attractive cover for the fish over a variety of water temperatures which they like.

- In locating your fish attractor, the initial step is to contact the authorities and check out any regulations or restrictions for depositing brush in the water. There are places in most lakes or rivers where a sizeable brushpile could create a navigation hazard. In some lakes, like the TVA-controlled reservoirs, permission must be obtained from the lake manager before sinking a brushpile. Normally, the authorities are quite happy to see you put out fish-attracting structures, and will offer both encouragement and sound advice on optimum locations. Your local Game Wardens can and will do the same.

- If available, purchase a topo map of the lake or river and take it with you when you sink your crappie condo. The map, plus your depthfinder (if the water is up) will enable you to find the necessary natural migration routes the fish follow; ie: channels, ditches, long ridges, old roadbeds, etc. When you sink your brushpile, mark the spot on your map, then make a few careful notes on the map itself about distinct landmarks on shore for future reference.

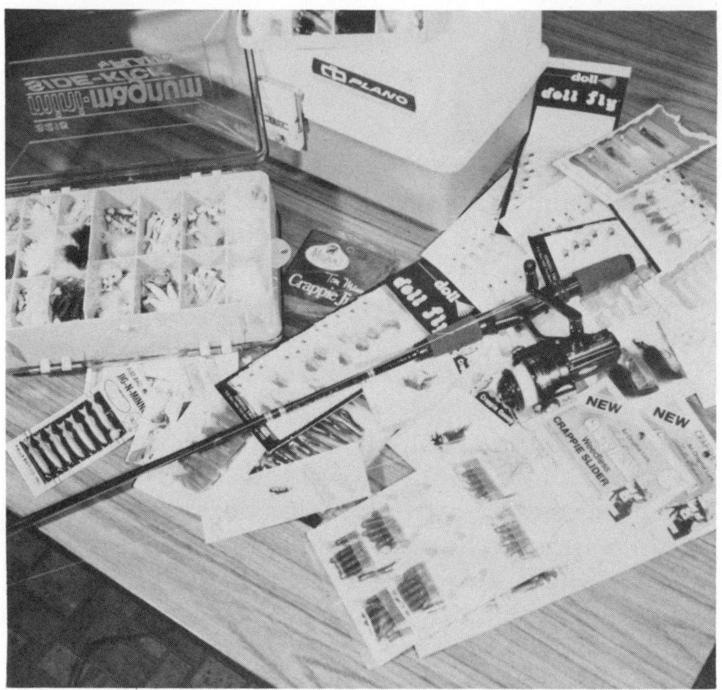

There is little doubt jigs are an extremely effective bait for taking crappie. Experiment with size, depth and speed of your retrieve.

- I have used Uncle Josh pork rind for years to add a bit of extra appeal to my artificial baits. It works well on crappie, too. Put a small "Ripple Rind" on your jigs, a "Little Vee" on spinners, or a "Fly Flick" on your popping bugs. Pork rind is a proven boost to your success.

- Remember: fish are *always* responsive to changes in water temperature. To be successful, you *must* remember that, and change your tactics when water temperatures change even slightly.

- Far too many crappie are missed because people literally don't know when they get a bite. Fishing with cork floats, observing the float move off and disappear under the surface is an obvious tip-off, but when tight-lining for crappie or casting a jig, it's quite different. Set the hook firmly (not strongly) the very instant you feel a tap. Crappie are generally not aggressive when they take a bait, and the light "pecks" or "taps" are frequently all the indication you have when the fish has your bait in its mouth. If you don't lift your rod or pole at that moment, the fish will often spit the bait.

- If you're enjoying a lakeside fish fry, the easiest way to tell when the grease in the skillet is hot enough to drop in your fish is to use a sulfur-tip match. Simply touch the head of the match to the surface of the grease. When it ignites, the grease is the right temperature for frying fish!

- Hooking the minnow correctly depends upon how you are fishing. If you're not moving, hook the minnow in the back, being careful not to injure his spine. He'll give more action when hooked that way. If you're fishing in current, or moving with the trolling motor, hook the minnow thru the lips (bottom to top) or thru the eyes. In this manner, he won't double up or spin as you move.

- At the time of this writing, there is a lot of enthusiasm (and skepticism) about liquid formulas designed to enhance the appeal of your bait to fish. One particular variety of the stuff, Fish Formula II, has been endorsed openly by several of the more-respected professional fishermen, and even attributed to several tournament wins. I tried it on crappie jigs, and caught more fish than my partner in the boat who was not using the scent on his offerings. Other fishermen I know and respect have tried the formula with similar results. It's well worth a go, and available from Keeper Bait Company, P.O. Box 158, Hollow Rock, TN 38342.

- Try tipping your jig or small spinner with very small pieces of fish, or with a minnow. You can cut little strips of meat (leave the skin on) from the belly flap or rib cage of crappie you have caught. The added smell/taste increases your catch.

- Cut off your motor well before reaching the spot you want to fish. Drift or paddle (or use the trolling motor) into position to avoid spooking the fish. In very shallow water, a paddle approach is better than using the trolling motor.

- Once your fish is hooked, maintain steady pressure with the rod and don't allow any slack in the line. Because of the paper-like mouths crappie have, when you give them slack in the line the hook can simply fall out of the hole it has created. Don't "pump" the fish with up and down motions of the rod and reel, as this only enlarges the hole in its mouth. You can play with the fish after he's in the boat, not before.

- Don't remain in the same spot for long if you haven't gotten a bite. Especially in shallow water, it doesn't take but a few minutes for the fish to take your bait. Lack of attention means you need to try another cast, or drop your minnow on the other side of the stump. In deeper water (and colder water), you do indeed have to have more patience and leave your offering in the same place for longer times.

- When the action is slow, switch to smaller lures or minnows.

- Color is a highly-debated subject for jigs used on crappie. Generally, white, black and yellow are the most popular. Black is usually best in murky waters. The fluorescent colors often spark action, especially pink and green. Jigs with flash (tinsel wrap or spinner blades) are quite good, except in very clear water.

- When minnow fishing, a bright gold hook, small spinner blades and red beads on the rig often increase your catch.

- When the action slows it doesn't necessarily mean you have caught all the fish in the area! Move only a short distance away, or change depths about two feet with your bait. Often you'll find the fish this way, and continue taking them handily.

- When jig fishing around stumps, piers or bridge pilings, cast *beyond* the structure and allow your jig to sink a bit before starting the retrieve. In this manner your jig will be the correct depth as it passes by the structure. Otherwise, you will have pulled the bait past the productive area before it had time to sink into the right depth for action.

Finding a school of crappie holding on or near a brush pile usually produces fast action.

- When fishing with jigs and the action slows, change color immediately. Crappie sometimes "get wise" to a particular color, and changing it will allow you to continue catching them in the same place.

- Work your minnow all around the edges of a brushpile before trying to place it into the center. You'll pick up several on the outer edges before chancing a hang-up in the center which spooks the fish.

Shallow-water crappie fishing often generates fast action, too.

- Weather and water conditions affect fish in deep water far less than those in shallow water. If you have found a pattern in the deeper water areas, chances are it will remain productive for days. Shallow-water patterns can change in a matter of hours.

- It's not enough to succeed on good days. You should be able to know *why* you succeeded. Study and ask questions. On those fishless days, figure out why they were unsuccessful and make them work for you by analyzing what went wrong. The very best tactics for catching crappie consistently come from between your ears. Watch, observe, think and apply what you learn. Take notes.

• When you try and fail to catch crappie, there are *only three* probable causes to deal with: 1) you're not fishing where the fish are at that moment; 2) you're using the wrong size bait or retrieving it at the wrong speed; or 3) you're fishing at the wrong depth. You can catch crappie every week of the year if you will only experiment with the above three possibilities until you find the right combination.

• The depth you are fishing is almost always the most critical part of your success or failure.

• Even on days when you're catching fish, it's wise to experiment with different types/sizes of bait. Often you can take considerably more fish by changing to a smaller minnow, or switching from a 1/32 oz. jig to a 1/64 oz. Those who use their head and experiment on the water are the ones local people tag as the experts.

• Those dreary, overcast days are far better for fishing success than the clear, "Bluebird" ones.

• In early springtime, don't overlook the opportunity to take really fine stringers of crappie in the spillways below your local dam. Crappie very often move upstream in March or early April as they begin searching for a place to spawn. When they reach the dam, they congregate and mill around the area for a while, and you have an excellent opportunity for some outstanding catches there.

- During the hot summer weather, crappie often locate themselves in places which offer them some shade and relief from the sun's glare. Try fishing under piers, docks and bridges. Also, the bases of larger stumps can offer them some shade, so work your bait around into the shaded side of such structure.

- Crappie move around a lot, even though they generally travel in large schools most of the year. If you have a favorite spot in the appropriate part of the lake for the season you're fishing, but find no fish there, keep trying back from time to time. Chances are, the fish will move in there. Also, after catching a few fish at one place until the action slows, come back to it later, as those fish or another bunch will probably have moved back onto the structure.

- Sloughs, cut-outs and large ditches which offer cover and a five-to-eight-foot drop-off are excellent places to find crappie in the fall. These are natural migration routes, and the cover will hold good amounts of food for them, thus making these places highly productive.

Where To Find 'Em Year-Round

During the really cold months of January and February, crappie hold in the deeper waters of the lake or rivers. They do little feeding during this time, their slowed metabolism making them require lesser amounts of food for survival. You will find them on sloping drop-offs where water depths go from shallow to very deep, especially in the larger bays and mouths of the larger creeks.

Toward the latter part of February and the first of March, crappie migrate a short distance from these deeper water haunts into the mouths of the creeks and smaller bays (or further into the larger ones). The first place they go there is to the ridges, humps and underwater islands. They are plentiful at this time, and the ridges which feature deep drop-offs on one or more sides are the most productive spots for several weeks in March. They are still reasonably inactive, so you must use the lightest tackle possible to detect the faint taps which signal a crappie bite in the still-cold water. However, it's an excellent time to fish for them.

In April the crappie begin moving around looking for places to spawn. They go to the bushes, stumps, various kinds of wooden structure, weed beds and underwater weed points, scattering all over the place in the more shallow waters. Larger minnows and jigs can be used now, as the fish are much more active. While it is true huge numbers of crappie are spending their efforts along the banks in April, an equally large number, and usually the larger fish, can be found in the eight-to-ten-foot waters slightly offshore. Look for drops and brush in these depths and you'll probably encounter the best springtime action you've ever had.

May is sometimes a tough month for crappie catching. After spawning, they seem to wander at random, showing up for lunch at one place, tak-

A cork float on the line allows a variety of retrieves and/or controlled depths. (Photo courtesy TVA)

ing supper somewhere else. You have to hunt for them a bit more in May, but concentrate on the open-water humps near the creek channels and you'll usually catch them in good numbers.

June and July bring warmer weather, warmer water. Crappie begin their migration back out into the main parts of the lake. June finds them hanging around the creek and river mouths to some extent, but by July they have set up housekeeping all along the old river channel out in the middle of the lake. This is not to say every crappie in the area will be out there, but the majority will be, and especially the larger ones.

Most people claim the hot months of July and August are the worst for crappie fishing. Actually, this the time you can find them with the most ease. They definitely are to be found on the river channels in deeper water, holding along the shoulder in 12 to 25-foot depths. You can take crappie there at almost any hour of the day. Probably the best spot is where the bottom comes up from 40 or 50 feet out in the main channel to about 15 feet on the top of the shoulder.

Crappie make another migration towards shore in September. Depending upon temperatures, and how long they remain constant, the fish first go back to the bays and larger creek mouths, similar to where you found them in March. Creek and river mouths offering underwater ridges usually host great numbers of crappie in September and early October. The action can be exceptionally good at this time of year. Often, again depending on the water temperatures and how long they remain constant, crappie will go right into the shallow water during the fall months. You can find them in three-to-four-foot dep-

Constructed at home and taken to the lake, stake beds can provide excellent "hot spots" for crappie action. (Photo courtesy H. Lea Lawrence)

ths and have a ball!

November and December are virtually unheard- of-months for catching crappie in most of the country. Barring limitations imposed by hard water (ice), there is one technique which works quite well at this time. When it's really cold, crappie usually feed up into shallower water at least once a day. The trick is to find some five-foot water which has a medium slope drop-off next to it going down to at least 30 feet. It's almost a sure bet you can find crappie somewhere on that slope day after day during the Holiday Season. The fish stay there from the latter part of November all the way thru January and February. Find a drop-off fitting the description near the mouth of a creek or river, then work your bottom rig slowly up and down the slope until you find the productive zone.

Month	**Location/Procedure**
January and February	Deeper water on sloping drop-offs where depths go from shallow to very deep. Very slow presentation using very small minnows or jigs. Concentrate on areas in the larger bays of the lake and mouths of the larger rivers or creeks. Average depth varies along the drop-offs, depending on water temperatures.
Mid-February thru March	Crappie migrate into the mouths of the creeks and a bit further towards shore in the large bays. They go to the underwater ridges and humps and stay there for several weeks. Best bets are ridges which offer a deep drop-off on one or both sides. This is an excellent time to catch them, but you still need light tackle to detect the faint bites in cold water.
April	Starting to look around for places to spawn, crappie head for the shoreline, seeking a variety of structure, including almost anything wooden and an assortment of vegetation like weed beds (cabbage weed in northern states). They will be found in much more shallow

water near the shoreline, but many remain in water around the 10-foot depth and can be caught there easily as they may spawn in the deeper areas, or be passing thru either coming to or going from the shoreline areas. Larger minnows and jigs are appropriate now, as the fish are more active and aggressive.

May   In mid-America, the spawning run is in full swing early in the month. Further south, it probably has peaked; further north perhaps just beginning. Continue searching the shallows around various types of structure, and also the drop-offs in 8 to 10-foot water. In areas where the spawn is ending, the crappie will be found randomly wandering and moving almost constantly. Be sure to concentrate on the drop-offs and creek channels, ditches, etc. slightly out away from shore, as these are the routes the fish will be taking for the most part. Open-water humps and ridges are excellent places to work after the spawn.

June and July   As the water warms, the crappie will begin their migration back out into the main lake in mass. First they go back out into the mouths of the creeks and bays, then on out to the old river channel in the middle of the lake. Work the deeper drop-offs and along the shoulder of the main river channel in the 12 to 25-foot range.

July and August

Crappie are definitely on the river channel edges out in the main lake. They are quite easy to find now, and will bite at practically any hour of the day. Night fishing with lanterns under bridges and around rip-rap near the channels is an excellent way to enjoy good catches. Best spots are where bottom comes up from 40 or 50 feet in the channel to about 15 feet on the shoulder.

September and October

Depending upon water temperatures as the weather moderates in fall, crappie make a move back in towards shore. They move back to the mouths of the larger creeks and bays on the ridges and underwater humps, similar to where they were holding in March. If the weather holds relatively stable, they may go further into the shallower-water structure in the four or five-foot depths.

November and December	When the water really gets cold, crappie make another shift in location, although only slight in distance. They back up a bit from the shallower structure and move a short distance out into the lake where they find slopes and drop-offs which offer them a combination of both very deep water on one side, and rather shallow water on the other. They stay there all the way thru January and most of February. Fish for them as suggested above for those months.

Apply what you have read on techniques in any month of the year, and you should come home with healthy tablefare. (Photo courtesy Kentucky Tourism)

5

Practical Applications

Winter

Snowflakes were swirling around in the air. More than a few found their way down the back of my collar; others lit briefly on the tip of my nose. Despite the lack of proper clothing and the absence of gloves which caused shivering and foot-stomping on the bank, I paid only slight attention to the weather situation.

I stood several feet back from the bank, peering over the edge, eyes riveted to the tiny cork float on my line drifting slowly past the three stumps in the water. Rarely did the float make it past the second stump before it silently disappeared from sight into the gray/green water. Repeatedly, the heavy pull on the line promised another good fish for the cooler.

My good friend Al Adams and I were experiencing the rewards of being in the right place at the right time. We were catching crappie almost as fast as we could stick a minnow on the hook and

Winter catches like this are possible when you know how and where to find the fish.

toss it into the slow-moving creek. Big crappie. Lots of big crappie.

The day began with a morning of welcome sunshine during the dreary days of January in central Kentucky. It happened to come on a Saturday, and Al and I promised our wives a fun day of picnicing in the moderating weather. We selected a public picnic area near home on the edge of a small creek. I "forgot" the soft drinks, remembering same just as we passed by a local grocery store that also happened to sell minnows. By sheer coincidence, I had misplaced a couple of cane poles and a small tacklebox in the back of the pickup truck. Taking advantage of the situation, we purchased a few dozen minnows along with the soft drinks.

We didn't catch any fish at first, but it was a grand picnic anyway. Until the weather changed abruptly and it began spitting snow. The ladies picked up the loose goodies on the table, Al helped them gather stuff and carry it to the truck, and I went over to the bank to pick up the cane poles before leaving. Both poles had been unattended for some time. Both cork floats were somewhere out of sight beneath the surface. And both rigs had a crappie on the other end.

Our wives occupied the truck with the heater running for the next hour or more. Occasionally, they rolled down a window momentarily to make comments on our sanity and/or their state of boredom. No matter. Al and I both grunted repeatedly as we eventually carried our crappie-filled ice chest up the snow-covered hill to the parking lot. We had considered asking our wives to go purchase more minnows, except we feared they might not come back.

Why did we hit the action so perfectly? Why didn't we catch crappie initially when we tried?

The very sudden change in conditions apparently sparked a feeding frenzy, perhaps catching the fish off-guard as it did us. When the sunshine went away and the front started moving into the area, (it snowed like blue blazes for almost 18 hours after we got home) the fish moved up the slope of the drop-off where we were fishing, and began feeding actively. It just so happened the picnic table we selected in the empty camp ground was next to those three stumps near the top of the drop-off. The crappie had been further down the slope all the time, and just out of range for our minnows when we began fishing. The weather change made them come up to feed and our baited hooks did the rest of the job in providing several fine meals afterwards.

Crappie are typically slow-moving in cold water. They require less food for survival, and won't chase a minnow or jig any distance at all. But they still eat. When they do take it, the bite is very faint, making it tough to realize they have the bait in their mouth. Sometimes in extreme cases, you have to lift your rod or pole to see if there's a crappie on the other end! The episode described above is the only time I have ever seen winter crappie take minnows with any degree of enthusiasm. Normally, they are less energetic than a fishworm after an hour in a bucket of ice cubes.

Cold water is a relative description, depending upon where you do your wintertime fishing. In northern states, the cold water has a tendency to turn solid for several inches on the surface. In Florida or southern Texas, cold water can mean you may need a T-shirt to go water-skiing on Christmas Day if you get wet. Regardless, the changes in temperature between summer and winter will affect the crappie in similar fashion. They definitely slow down their activity somewhat. Smaller baits, slower action on your part, and patience while waiting on the fish to bite are required.

Crappie taken in winter months offer a bonus in the tablefare department. The flavor is better, and the flesh more firm. While many anglers shun the cold, harsh conditions typical of December, January and February, many others I know would rather stock their freezers with crappie at that time than any other. And it's a sure bet the lake won't be crowded!

"Bottom bumping" in cold weather can be quite productive. (Photo courtesy TVA)

You'll find crappie relate to structure in winter months just as they do any other time. But their feeding time may vary slightly. I have found crappie generally can be taken at any hour of the day; some periods more readily than others, of course. However, winter crappie, esepcially as you travel northward, seem to get on the "early and late" kick. Some of my good Yankee pals say they only go out early morning and late evening. I have no explanation for this; it does not hold true in my local waters of Kentucky and Tennessee. We sometimes catch them from floating duck blinds during the mid-day lull in shooting!

Finding the fish in winter can present a problem. This is especially true when we have a mild season, or one with many fluctuations in temperature. The winter of 1982-83 was just such a season in my area. Both December and January were mild months, sporting only a token amount of snow and providing some welcome relief on heating bills across the state. The crappie couldn't quite figure out what was going on, as one day the sun would shine, warming the shallows, then by the weekend there might be a bit of ice skimming the stick-ups.

We caught crappie in 25-foot water along deep drop-offs. We also caught them handily one December morning close to the banks in only three-foot water. Their own environment kept changing on them frequently, so they merely reacted to the stimuli by changing their depth frequently. All fish do this pretty routinely. Their behavior patterns are *rigidly* controlled by their environment. It's worth noting the behavior patterns of the crappie's food sources are also controlled by that same environment.

The point here is that a change in temperature, bright sunshine followed by rain or snow, a rise or fall in the water level, and a host of other variables generate responses from fish. When the stimuli they receive remain relatively constant, the fish live their life in a relatively constant manner. If winter sets in and water temps become stable where the fish are holding, they will position themselves at a certain depth and stay there until things change. Find them one day at 20 feet, and barring changes in their surroundings, the fish will be right there the following day. Once you find winter crappie, you should be able to stay with them and do quite well.

There is one key to finding these fish in cold weather which will help. If you can find a jumbo-size underwater point which slopes gradually out into the lake, you're probably in business. The ideal point will offer the crappie a wide choice of water depths; ie: they can travel the slope from very deep water out at the end, all the way up into very shallow water. Underwater islands and/or ridges featuring the same wide range of bottom depth are also great places to find winter crappie. These places are like magnets, offering the fish an easy way out in responding to changing stimuli. They can move up the slope to feed or warm themselves on sunny days, or back down a few yards on days when things are cold and glum. (In summer, they move up on the overcast days, go deeper when it's bright and sunny.)

Finding a sloping bottom area going from very deep to very shallow is your best ticket for winter success on crappie. Your job becomes one of eliminating non-productive depths until you hit the fillet zone. Simply work up and down the point until you find them. As mentioned, crappie aren't going to jump all over your bait when they're shivering in that cold water, so you'll have to be patient and realize the tiny pecks and nibbles at your minnow or jig are actually fish trying to eat lunch without taking their hands out of their pockets.

The double-hook rig described for "bottom bumping" or tight-lining is an excellent choice for working cold winter waters up and down slopes. You might speed the process by tying another hook or two above the basic pair, covering more depths with each pass. If you prefer using a cork float, you can spider-leg a number of poles around the boat at different depths while working slowly up or down the area. You'll need mini floats, however, to register the faint hits on the bait. Use the long, skinny ones that require practically no muscle to sink, or maybe rig up

Deep-water catch taken in November proves knowledge of where the fish will be holding is the key to success. (Photo courtesy TVA)

some old fashioned porcupine quills to use as floats.

Fishermen in the northern states are faced with either a real problem, or a real opportunity for fun when winter freezes over their favorite fishing spots. Depends on how you look at it. Ice fishing is both popular and productive for taking winter crappie. It also borders on lunacy in the minds of some southern anglers who may not have tried it for themselves.

Actually, ice fishing in the northern states is one of the very best methods for catching crappie in winter. Not only do you bring in a good mess of fish, you also typically enjoy the company of other hearty types out there braving the cold to fish thru the "hard" water. Sometimes the whole day turns into a semi-social event as groups form over feeding fish and everyone shares in the fun.

Common sense will tell you spending the day on ice requires adequate clothing. If you're not dressed warmly, it's unlikely even the best of action can keep you happy for more than an hour or two. Hard to have a good time when you're shivering. As the tackle and techniques are fairly simple, it's safe to say the single-most important part of ice fishing is your own personal comfort. Waterproof, insulated boots are keenly important, as are truly good gloves or mittens, a quality item of headgear, and perhaps a down vest worn beneath several layers of outerwear. You may sweat like a pony walking out to your fishing spot, or tugging along a sled filled with your tackle. But once you're there, you'll thank the stars for the extra layers of clothes. While exerting yourself physically going and coming from the fishing hole, remove some of the layers. Once there, put on the extra goodies to preserve body heat.

Selecting the location where you will drill or cut the hole in the ice is rather critical. In Michigan, for example, many of the lakes are fairly shallow with a few distinct drop-offs in the bottom configuration. If you can locate yourself just above one of those drop-offs, you're in business. If not, you play the "hit or miss" game that day. If you have a good idea of the lake bottom contours before freeze-up, you may be able to line up landmarks on the shore which you previously made a note of in finding the drops. Working eight-to-twenty-foot water in these shallow lakes seems best. If you find weeds below, they come as a bonus.

If you have one of the portable depthfinders on

the market, you may be surprised to learn they will definitely solve your problems in locating your spot over a drop-off. Yep. They can shoot a signal thru the ice slick as a sled track. Here's how:

First, clean away any snow on the ice, where you want to take a look-see at bottom with your sonar machine. A six or seven-inch circle will do nicely. Clear and scrape the surface until you get down to clean ice, making the area as smooth as you can in the little circle. Pour a small quantity of antifreeze, which you just happen to have with you, onto the ice in the circle. Place the transducer into the small puddle of nofreezum and flip on the switch. Easy! Continue moving a little at a time if you're near the predicted drop-off, until you find it with the depthfinder. If you're just shooting blind in hopes of locating a change in bottom, move longer distances between trying the sonar. "Fine tune" the location after you discover a material change in depth between readings. A handwarmer placed into the container for the unit's battery will make it happy, and it won't lose its juice so quickly in the cold temperatures.

Sometimes you run into situations where the ice has either thawed and refrozen, or shifted and split. In either case, the depthfinder may not be able to perform properly because there is air trapped in the ice. Depthfinders cannot shoot a signal thru air. Move a bit until you find solid ice.

Once you have selected the spot for setting up shop on the ice, the next chore is to drill a six or eight-inch hole thru the stuff. Ice augers are somewhat expensive, but are very effective in saving time and sore muscles. To cut a hole in

Depthfinders definitely can perform thru the ice, if you know how.

reasonably thick ice, you need either an ice auger or two men and a bottle of whiskey to chop the hole.

Fishing the open lake without benefit of an ice house or shanty, try to stay back at least a foot from the opening at all times. When you chop a hole in the ice, it lets a ray of light enter the water below. Crowding around the hole above, you block the light, creating moving shadows which can spook the fish. The noise you make on the ice seems to have little effect on the fish. But those shadows moving across the opening sure as heck affect them!

If you have a shanty for ice fishing, the hole usually can be cut somewhat larger, allowing two or more people to fish thru it at the same time. A lantern is usually hung near the water surface, providing both the fish-attracting light below, and the people-attracting warmth inside the shanty. Of course, those bench seats, Coleman stoves and steaming coffee pots are pretty neat comforts, too.

Most ice anglers use specialized tackle perfectly suited to the conditions. A tiny, short rod, usually of limber fiberglass, is used to detect the light taps from fish. A small reel is fixed to the rod for holding and adjusting the line. Some use very small floats; most prefer to tight-line with a small sinker on the line. Hooks are generally smaller and have shorter shanks than those used in warm weather crappie fishing. A few ingenious ice fishermen rig up a piece of thin steel wire, taping one end to the rod a few inches from the tip, and forming a small loop in the other. The line is run thru the eyes of the rod, thru the loop in the wire, and then thru the eye on the rod tip. Even the smallest and lightest bite on the bait will cause the thin wire to bob up and down. I believe you can purchase a similar deal in many of the stores nowdays, too.

The most popular bait for ice fishing is an active live minnow. Try to keep your line centered in the hole, preventing the loss of tackle if the line rubs and frays against the ice too much. Using minnows, you'll likely pick up a few other species of fish during the day, and some of them don't want to come straight up thru the hole! Corn worms, wax worms, "mousies," and grubs are all good baits to use when ice fishing.

My good friend, Bob Lancina, used to live in one of the northern states, and did a great deal of ice fishing. Successful trips on the ice were pretty

A fine mess of crappie taken from deep water drop-offs. (Photo courtesy TWRA)

routine. Bob also did a fair amount of scuba diving beneath the ice, and his observations from both above and below the surface are revealing. Bob says:

"The art to ice fishing is not in the catching of fish, but in *finding the right place to fish*. Fishing along drop-offs is excellent most of the time, day or night, and if you happen to hit one with weeds in the area, so much the better.

"Probably because of the critical oxygen supply in the water when the lake freezes, you'll almost always find a good concentration of fish around underwater springs, entrances of creeks into the lake, or where a small stream flows beneath the surface. These spots usually have to be found and marked before the freeze-up so you can return there to fish. I knew one fella up home who knew exactly the location of a large underwater spring in our local lake. He was consistently the first man on the ice every year, pushing his shanty out there on the thin ice to be sure he got the spot before anyone else. The man wore a wet suit when he did it, just in case the ice gave way! But he caught fish there every day he went. All winter. Every winter I was there.

"Diving below the ice revealed the water is three or four times more clear when the lake is frozen. There obviously are no boats or skiers churning up the particles, and you wouldn't believe how clean and clear things get under the ice. If there is much snow on the ice, the hole you cut lets in a great deal of sunlight, too. And because of the clear water, you'll need small diameter line."

Occasionally, Bob may have sunk a brush pile near either a small spring or a good drop-off prior to winter. Placing a shanty atop one of those "hot spots" surely could do wonders for the weight of your stringer. Also, fishermen who own the small, portable ice houses or pop-up tents usually are quite successful because they can and do move about when the fishing is slow. Frequently, you can find good action only a short distance from the spot you're sitting over and having little luck working. Change depths often until you hit. If nothing works there, move to a new spot.

Begin fishing only a foot or so off bottom, and continue to bring the bait upwards at reasonable intervals until you find the fish. If you don't have a depthfinder to find a drop-off, and you don't know the lake, try looking for other ice fishermen on the lake! They're a great bunch, and they'll almost always help you.

Another non-typical method for taking winter crappie which can produce excellent stringers of fish comes courtesy of the electric company in many areas. When you have a power plant built on the river, it often produces great quantities of super-hot water in the process of creating electricity. This water is conveniently dumped back into the river, raising the water temperature materially for quite some distance downstream from the discharge point. Fish of all species take advantage of this escape from wintertime cold water, seeking out their own preferred comfort zone.

Water entering the river at the discharge point is far too hot for the fish to enjoy. However, as you travel further downstream and the hot stuff mixes with the otherwise cold water, the blend forms a wide variety of temperature zones. Like a magnet, these comfort zones draw the fish and concentrate them for you.

A couple of words of caution are needed. First, there can be an element of danger involved when motoring your boat in too close to the discharge. If so, the area is generally marked clearly, and boat traffic is not allowed. Mind the signs. Secondly, if the power plant is one of those "on again, off again" deals, the discharge may be doing more harm than good for your winter fishing. Fish experience a fatal trauma, called temperature shock, when the water changes rapidly up or down in degrees.

At any rate, fishing below the hot-water discharge of power plants can prove delightfully rewarding on the suppertable. You no doubt will catch a variety of fish species there, too.

The Game Warden pressed the key on his radio mike. "Harry, you better come take a look at this one," he said with a frown, nodding in my direction. Then he returned to my boat, walking around it once more, intently checking out every detail. Moments later, the second law enforcement official arrived, idling his boat to a stop at the ramp.

It was the dead of winter in Tennessee. Some passing hunters saw the two wardens giving my boat the once-over, and they stopped to see what was going on. What had begun as a routine license check was developing into a crowd-drawing event.

One of the hunters voiced the typical reaction of everyone in the group when he saw the size-

In low water periods, sink brush along drop-offs and natural migration routes the fish will follow. (Photo courtesy TWRA)

able stringer of fish. "I don't believe this! Nobody around here catches crappie like that in January!" he blurted out, his breath hanging in the cold air.

"Whatnhell did you use for bait, a perch-colored hand grenade?" another man joked. (The wardens didn't think that was particularly humorous.)

I explained that I had been given a magazine article to do on winter crappie fishing techniques, and wanted to prove they worked prior to releasing the copy to the editor. Obviously, the tips I planned to share with his readers would work. This seemed to resolve the matter temporarily. Then the inevitable rush of questions began: "Where did you find them? How deep? What bait? How did you find them?" etc.

Answers to their questions, and the meat of the

article I wrote, went something like this:

Most fishermen really lose the crappie in December and January. Fishing conditions get pretty tough. Uncomfortable. On many days the spirit is willing, but the body says to heck with it, preferring to remain inside by the fire. But if you're the hearty type and can enjoy fishing in the cold, you can take advantage of the predictable movement pattern crappie will make at this time of year.

Migration patterns which crappie follow in spring, summer and fall are fairly substantial, often covering a material change in depth and a fair distance across the lake bottom as they move from one place to another. Now the crappie move much less. But they still move up and down in depth.

When the water gets quite cold and it's almost too miserable to be out on the lake, crappie will feed daily up into shallow water. However, their holding area will always be in or near much deeper water. If you can find water five or six feet deep which has a 25 to 35-foot drop-off right next to it, you'll find crappie on that slope in winter months almost without fail. Your job then becomes one of determining at which depth along the slope the fish are holding when you get there. Use any of the appropriate methods already described to do this, and once you locate them simply go to work right there.

The action is definitely slower than during warmer months, but it's predictable and dependable. Also, in the absence of frequent weather flip-flops, the crappie will remain on that type structure from the end of November all the way through February.

In summary, there are a number of points to consider for increasing your success on winter crappie:

Colder water will slow down the activity. Fish are cold-blooded, therefore when the water is cold they get cold, and thoughts of being frisky or playful never enter their minds. They do everything slowly and deliberately. You will need tackle of genuine sensitivity to detect the soft taps on the bait. Very limber poles or ultra-light gear with light line are needed.

In cold weather, use smaller minnows or jigs. Crappie will neither fight nor chase a large bait when their metabolism rate has shifted into low gear. They definitely will take a small bait over a larger one every time.

Weather changes have a noticeable effect on crappie. Just *before* a storm, crappie feed more actively. When the front hits, they stop feeding almost totally for the time being. A very light sleet or rain seems to perk them up a bit, and they bite well in lousy weather, providing the change is very gradual and steady. A light, steady drizzle generates very good fishing.

In man-made lakes, dropping the water level is very bad for crappie fishing action. Raising the water often improves your success. (This is more important in spring than winter, however.)

Crappie usually feed near the bottom. If you're not having much luck working the lower level, try coming up some three or four feet and you usually will find them there.

You know winter crappie are going to be off-shore and on the deep-water drop-offs. Check out river and creek channels which often feature shoulders covered with stumps at the desired

Tiny floats or sensitive tackle are needed to detect the faint bites from cold-weather crappie. (Photo courtesy Louisiana Wildlife & Fisheries Commission)

depths. Concentrate on the mouths of bays and creeks entering the lake. Underwater islands covered with brush are often ideal, and you can "doctor" these places yourself well in advance to produce excellent winter action.

Feel your way along slowly with the tight-line rig, or park your boat perpendicular to the drop-off and cast jigs. Vary depth/speed of retrieve which allows you to cover all the water before moving. Work either live or artificial baits very slowly.

When searching for correct depth, try letting a small jig or minnow go all the way to the bottom. Begin reeling in *very* slowly until you get a hit.

Winter crappie fishing can be great fun if you go about it correctly. The fish will cooperate willingly, and the tablefare is excellent when taken from the colder waters. Dress warmly, and enjoy this most-overlooked time of year for crappie fishing.

Spring

New life, fresh growth. You awaken one morning to a world of clean air, sweet odors and overnight buds on the trees and shrubs. The air is still chilly to the face, but the sunshine is *so* warm and comforting after a long winter of coldness. Birds, animals and fishermen begin their spring rituals with almost routine predictability.

Most of us have already cleaned and restocked tackleboxes, put new line on old reels, carefully sharpened hooks and given the battered jon boat

Brushy places in shallow water back up the creeks is an excellent place for spring crappie. (Photo courtesy John Phillips)

a good once-over cleaning. Some of us finally got around to repacking the trailer wheel bearings and emptying the old gas in our tanks left over from the last trip of fall. While teenage girls are shopping for bathing suits more revealing than their parents will enjoy seeing, we fishermen are bursting with anticipation over the first trip to the water in the new year. All is ready. We are prepared to reap the bounty of Nature as crappie charge the banks to spawn.

Trouble is, we're ready but the crappie probably aren't. As previously mentioned, fish are cold-blooded; they act and react to the various stimuli they receive from their environment.

Can you think of a *more changeble* time of year than spring?

Those few days of yellow, pink or white blooms on shrubs and flowers in the yard, coupled with sunshine and mild weather, are soon followed by another spree of spitting snow or cold rain. "April showers" often come in either March or May, and the dudes who control the locks and gates at your local reservoir get jumpy trying to predict the "summer pool" requirements. They raise and drop the water levels constantly by opening and closing the dam spillways.

Every time the sun shines, or it stops shining, the rains come, the water level rises or falls, the snows dump mini ice cubes in the lake, or the winds blow hard, the poor crappie are getting clobbered with different situations to which they react. And don't kid yourself, every time any of the above conditions comes along, *fish will move and change depth.* I've caught crappie in the shallows in early March one day, only to find them holding 100 yards off-shore on a drop

When crappie go to the banks to spawn, you'll find them in shallow water around structure.

somewhere the next day after a front moved thru the area during the night. Everybody goes to the shallow stuff in spring because they have been taught crappie will be there doing their thing once the winter weather goes away. It's true on some days, but definitely not a sure bet day after day in springtime. Don't overlook the fact shallow water is *much more affected* by weather changes than the deeper liquid.

Crappie are probably the least predictable in spring as compared to any other time of year.

Somewhere between early and late April, fishermen begin arriving at lakes en masse. Local residents offer advice, pass along "tips" on the latest action and proudly display Polaroid snapshots of yesterday's bounty. Bait shops with full shelves do a booming business as cash registers chime happily 14 hours a day, or maybe more. Tackle, bait, raingear and junk food sell like gangbusters as anxious fishermen stock up for a day of fun on the water hauling in crappie. On Kentucky Lake alone, spring fishermen purchase an estimated quarter-million minnows daily!

As temperatures warm the water in early spring, male crappie move towards the bank looking for stick-ups, stumps and any other variety of wooden structure. In the absence of wooden structure, they pick spots on hard-packed bottom (to avoid problems later with silt covering the eggs) and begin fanning out small, dish-shaped depressions in shallow-water areas. Sporting their darker spawning colors, males do the work in advance of the females' arrival, then wait there impatiently for the fun to begin. Days later, the girls hit town and things liven up considerably.

Several days of warm weather sparks the female crappie to move into the shallow water, preparing to lay her eggs. Then two days later the weatherman sends greetings from Canada and there is a cold front roaring thru the area. The females react by backing off into deeper water to think things over again. Cold snaps in spring are to female crappie like the question "What time do you get off, Honey?" to paid barmaids in your local pub. Both situations are frustrating to the males.

Days later, the female crappie may come back to the bank. Then the chaps who own a key to the dam gates decide it's time to drop the lake level in preparation for predicted rainfall during the following week. Again, the females respond to the situation by moving back out into deeper water. They don't like dropping water levels either, especially when they are about to lay eggs somewhere that might be on dry land before they hatch.

The various combinations of stimuli from weather and water changes will keep the crappie population in a continuing state of uproar for the four-to-twelve week period we call the annual spawning run. It becomes almost impossible to pinpoint exactly where the crappie will be, either in depth or location. They become scattered all over the place. You'll catch a braggin' stringer in 12-foot water while the next two boatsfull of guys kill them in places hardly knee deep.

It's a definite fact crappie will be going to the shoreline all during the spring to spawn. They'll be there *for sure*. But the trick is to discover where. Shallow? Suspended? On deeper drop-offs? And to complicate matters more, crappie move a lot during spring days and nights. You'll catch a basket of them in the morning, only to return to the spot after lunch and find it deserted. Predictable? No way!

Prior to the popularity of depthfinders and contour maps for fishermen, the only time crappie were caught in quantity was when the fish moved to the banks to spawn. Today, anglers can find underwater structure, drop-offs and creek channels out away from the shoreline and increase their success materially. Unfortunately, most people continue fishing for crappie in the spring just as their grandparents did, dipping minnows in the shallow water along shore into treetops, stuck-ups and stumps. Many times they find crappie there. Many times they don't.

Since crappie move unpredictably in spring, bank fishing often can become a matter of guesswork. Successful anglers must realize the fish move in and out routinely. When they have little luck fishing the shallows, these anglers move several yards out into the lake and work the deeper structure.

Jigs and spinners work quite effectively on crappie. When you exhaust your minnow supply, it surely doesn't mean you must head for the dock. Many of the better fishermen I know prefer artificials, and use them exclusively for crappie. Cast your small jigs into the bank and work them out slowly thru the stumps or stick-ups. Also cast around boat docks, piers, old barrels or anything wooden you find in the shallows. If you have problems losing jigs to snags, place a small float on the line above the lure and twitch or dance your bait back towards the boat at a depth which just

Share the fun with the youngsters. It'll make your days more meaningful. (Photo courtesy Bob Dennie)

clears the top of the brush. Vary the retrieve until you find what the crappie prefer in the way of action. It's a fantastically productive method.

As the spawning period draws to a close, drift fishing is probably one of the most effective methods for filling an ice chest with crappie. Many crappie will have completed their spawning activities and will be gradually making their way back out into the main lake. However, as all crappie don't spawn at the same time, many others may still be working their way into shore at that time. Drifting just offshore with several poles out can allow you to discover the route all these fish are taking as they migrate either in or out. When you pass over a school, anchor there and fish for a while. Areas around the mouths of creeks entering the lake are excellent places to try drift fishing at the end of the spawn.

Anytime you fish conventional structure unsuccessfully along the bank in springtime, you can logically assume the crappie have moved, at least temporarily, back out into slightly deeper water. When this happens, use your depthfinder to find some underwater drop-offs, ledges or tapering points near creek channels. The chances are extremely good your fish will be holding there for whatever reason. Depending on the weather and lake level, they may have moved back into shallow water by the next morning, so you'll have to do a bit of searching again to find them.

The biggest mistake crappie fishermen make is in trying to fish only one way during the spawning run.

If you're looking for the larger crappie instead of mere quantities of fish, I have found the majority of them will be caught in deeper water. Many

Stringers like this are what keep us going back time and again for more. (Photo courtesy Santee Cooper Country)

guides swear these "slab" crappie spawn in eight-to-ten-foot waters around the stumps. Most of the really good crappie I have taken over two pounds did indeed come from such places during the spawn. There is no question you can catch some of these big fish near shore when spring comes, but you'll catch many more if you move out slightly into deeper water and fish for them.

I use the double-hook outfit with 3/0 hooks, 15-pound line and a one-ounce lead sinker. It's surprising how often most of your fish will come from one hook, either the top or bottom one. Then the next day, it may reverse!

You'll need a very light, sensitive fiberglass pole to detect the crappie bites. You can certainly use floats, but "bottom bumping" or tight-lining is a better method because it gives you a superior sense of "feel" for the fish *and* structure below. Heavy tackle is a true handicap for crappie fishermen. There are times when crappie bite so gently you are unable to detect the hit with heavy poles which don't transmit the light taps to your findertips. When crappie fishing, the moment you feel a light tap, set the hook immediately. Don't wait for him to move off with the bait like a bass. Crappie and bulldoziers have very little in common.

You truly don't need expensive equipment to be successful fishing for crappie. Everyone, regardless of age or financial means, can enjoy the fun. Generally speaking, however, the spring crappie angler should remember the variety of weather he or she is likely to encounter. This means bringing sweaters and raingear to the lake with you, and it means the fish are also affected by changes which make it mandatory for you to move and vary your approach.

"Accuracy" is a term most often used by sportsmen describing bullet placement and shooting skills. Nobody talks about accurate fishing. But they should, especially when discussing crappie fishing. To score consistently on crappie, you must put your lure or minnow smack on the money every time. Failure to do so often means the pleasure is limited to a day on the water without tangible results for the table. The problem comes when crappie move around a lot and you can't see your "target."

Contrary to what most of us were taught, crappie do not come to the bank to spawn and remain there until they finish taking care of business. Many things cause them to move around. Understanding their behavior and their movement patterns is quite critical to your success. It allows you to place your bait where the schools of fish are now, not where they were yesterday.

When you're shoveling snow and cursing the high cost of keeping the house warm, crappie are sitting out in the deeper water of the lake, patiently waiting for spring. They are reasonably inactive, feeding with half-hearted efforts. They'll take a minnow with a soft, sucking action which gives the angler almost no indication he has a bite. Business is slow. You can catch plenty of crappie in winter months, but patience is gold plated. You almost have to "tease" crappie into biting your minnow or jig.

In early or mid-March, the initial waves of crappie begin moving. They migrate into the mouths of the creeks and smaller bays. The first place they will go is to the high ridges, humps and underwater islands there. Crappie are plentiful on these ridges, and the best place to find them is along the edge of the drop-offs of the structure where it goes into deeper water. The crappie remain there for several days, perhaps a week or more. The water is still very cold and they take your bait very gently. These cold-water fish are excellent eating because the meat is more firm and more tasty than at any other time of the

Brush piles sunk in the mouths of creeks usually produce well many months of the year.

year. It's a great time to fish for them. There is practically no competition from other anglers during the weeks immediately preceeding the magic day when everyone awakens to the reality "spring has sprung."

In April, everybody begins to get their act together. Crappie start moving away from the ridges in search of places to spawn. Fishermen optimistically clean out a corner of the family freezer they feel certain will be filled with fresh crappie fillets the following weekend. Bait shops inactive all winter suddenly boom and decide it's time to open the doors at five in the morning.

Tank trucks loaded with two-inch minnows rumble the back roads between boat docks. Phone lines are overloaded as winter-weary fishermen make plans to capitalize on the approaching action.

Tons of crappie are hauled in from shoreline structure. Countless tons of them go neglected just off-shore and never see a baited hook.

Routinely during the spring spawning time, crappie go to the shallow water and are found there around various types of structure. They scatter all over the lake or river, going to the banks where they seek treetops, stick-ups, stump beds, bushes, etc. During this egg-laying period, you can wade quietly along in the shallows, stand on the bank near brush, or fish right off the pier at boat docks and catch good stringers of fish. You would catch a lot more crappie, and larger ones, by working from a boat just a little further off shore.

All crappie don't decide to spawn at the same time. Neither do they all select the same depth water in which to lay their eggs. My own experiences indicate the larger fish prefer deeper water, maybe the eight-to-ten-foot stuff, for spawning. Many are the days when I have returned to the dock with either the same of slightly fewer numbers of spring crappie than the average angler brought in. But the ones I kept were nearly twice the size!

In addition to weather changes and fluctuations of the water levels which make crappie move back and forth between depths, imagine how long it would take 35 feeding crappie to exhaust the minnow population around any given piece of shoreline structure. When the food is devoured, those fish are going in search of a new lunch counter. They surely aren't gonna stay there telling themselves they would rather stand around waiting for a mate than eat. Sometime during the day, they'll move out on feeding safaries just to keep their strength up. Nobody enjoys making love when they haven't eaten for 48 hours! The need for food coupled with weather and water changes explains why crappie move around so much during the springtime. Anglers come back to the dock daily saying "they just aren't biting this afternoon." Truth is, they simply weren't putting their bait where the fish were that afternoon.

I began this mini-section with the word "accuracy." Basic as it may sound, accuracy in crappie fishing means putting your bait or jig into the school of fish, regardless of where they may be located at any given moment. Finding a brushpile, catching a few fish and then sitting there half the day waiting for the action to resume just won't get you any medals for accuracy. Neither will it fill your freezer.

Launch your boat and head for the mouth of a creek, a cove or small bay in the lake. Turn on your depthfinder as you approach one of these areas, and begin looking for a high ridge along the bottom. When you find one, fish it carefully. Maybe you'll find a new wave of crappie just arriving from the deeper water. You could discover where those larger crappie are holding who prefer spawning in deeper places. And you might find the bunch from the brushpile when they are out to lunch.

Work the ridges or humps completely, using the bottom-bumping technique previously described. Begin on the deeper, outside edge

Guide Steve McCadams adds another nice crappie to our mixed catch.

and gradually work up the side, over the top and down the inside drop. In the month of April you should catch crappie there without fail, almost without regard to weather conditions and water level, etc.

After covering the underwater ridge thoroughly and taking fish there until the action slows (if it does), you can start making your way into shore for more action. Follow the natural contour of the bottom as best possible; stay with the creek channel or drop-off as it runs into more shallow water. Present your bait or cast jigs in a fantail manner ahead of the boat. If you're fishing minnows and cane poles, put out two or three of them baited and set at slightly different depths beneath the floats. Move *slowly* with the trolling motor, or paddle along quietly. Stop every few feet to allow the minnow to catch up and hang motionless below the float for a couple of moments.

If you prefer tight-lining or casting small jigs, follow the same route toward shore, and present your bait over the greatest amount of bottom surface possible. You are searching for schools of feeding crappie between the deeper ridge and the bank, so the more water you can cover with your bait, the better chances you have of hitting the action. As the water becomes more shallow, your depthfinder becomes less effective in finding structure because of the reduced surface area it can read. You have to do the searching with your lure or minnow.

Somewhere between the two areas (ridge and bank) you are almost guaranteed to find feeding crappie, providing you go thru this exercise slowly and quietly. When you find fish, a small floating marker can be slipped into the water as a reference point. Then you can either remain there to fish, or circle the boat around to continue casting. I prefer to keep the boat moving gradually, even if in loose circles. Many people anchor right on the spot. Matter of preference, I guess, but I think you'll probably find more feeding fish if you keep moving. They are pretty scattered during this situation, and moving to and from the bank.

The final step in this procedure, of course, is to continue your move all the way into the shore. There you should begin picking up fish in the brushtops, stumps, etc. Just don't spend the day there! Take your fish as long as the action is good, then ease back out toward the underwater ridges again and start all over. There obviously will be times during this "search and move" routine when you are in unproductive water. But following the general route the fish themselves will be taking at this time certainly allows you to spend a far greater percentage of your time putting your bait accurately into schools of feeding spring crappie. There's no doubt about that point.

One of the neat things about fishing for crappie during their spring migration into shore is that they are coming off a period of relative inactivity in the cold, deeper water where they spent the winter. They're hungry. The spawning activity requires more food consumption than sitting out in the middle of the lake somewhere doing nothing. And as the water temperatures rise, the fish's metabolism rate picks up, making them more hungry, more active, etc. Normally, spring crappie will take any bite-sized offering you happen to put in front of their noses.

Crappie take jigs and minnows well almost any time of the day or night when you find them. (Photo courtesy TWRA)

Spring crappie present one of the best opportunities for the ultra-light enthusiast to truly enjoy himself. There are a great many fine mini-reels and tiny rods on the market which indeed maximize the fun when a good crappie jumps on your bait. Using two or four-pound line and a 1/32-oz. jig, you're in for a real ball when you cast around shallow structure into a bunch of hungry crappie! Cast to the outside edge of the treetops or sunken brush to avoid disturbing the branches or losing your jig if you get snagged. Use of a Palomar knot is recommended when you tie on your jig with the light mono.

Once you master the "search and move" method for spring crappie fishing, your success rate will climb materially, and the chances are definitely in your favor for catching more of the larger fish. Accuracy counts in fishing, too.

To summarize: spawning crappie are unpredictable. They move. They change depth. And they often frustrate the fisherman who knows or uses only one method for catching them. If you want to increase your stringer weight substantially when after spring crappie, use the "search and move" technique.

If you're in a new, unfamiliar area, begin by talking to the marina operators, as they are businessmen and want to see you come back again. They will give you the straight poop. Then buy a topo map of the lake. Look for the flat areas near shore which probably were fields prior to the lake impoundment. If not previously cultivated, these flat areas probably had woods on them at one time. Stumps remain on the bottom for a long time after flooding. Rather shallow, flat bays in many lakes are better producers than the really deep ones. If you can find a cut, channel or ditch running thru the flat, it's a genuine hotspot worth trying.

Select your spot, then begin fishing some 100 yards from shore, initially positioning the boat in about 12-foot water. Work your way towards shore, following the drop-off if you can. When you hit fish, set up shop and begin loading the boat. Use several poles, or cast to "fan" the area. Return to the 12-foot spot and approach the bank at a slightly different angle if unsuccessful on the first try.

You *will* find spring crappie in this manner.

Summer

From mid-June thru mid-September, when the scorching sun could blister a baseball, crappie fishing is excellent. These fish are more predictable at this time than at any other in the year. Your tennis shoes smell like catfish bait, your T-shirt and shorts are wet with perspiration, and the sun-tan lotion flows freely. But crappie are concentrated and quite willing to take your minnow or lure virtually anytime you offer it to them. In direct contrast to popular opinion, summer is the easiest time of all to catch great stringers of crappie.

"Darn. That's about it for this year, I guess," one angler says to the other.

"Yep. Guess the crappie have finished their spawning run and it's all over," the other replies

Stringers like this taken in the heat of summer can cause quite a stir at the local dock! (Photo courtesy John Phillips)

after a fruitless day working the banks. "Wonder if the dude at the bait shop will buy all these minnows back?"

That's a fairly typical exchange between crappie fishermen who feel the only time to catch their fish is when they come to the banks to spawn in the spring. Most people will take a crack at filling their freezer with crappie during the fairly short period when the fish are busy with their egg-laying routine as the weather warms after a long, cold winter. Once that activity is over, the vast majority of crappie fishermen seem to feel their favorite species suddenly vanishes into the unknown.

Crappie eat more often than once a year.

Unfortunately, most anglers suffer from the old adage, "Fish don't bite much in hot weather." Crappie do. Vacation plans are made annually in warmer months which include a variety of water sports like skiing, swimming and sun-bathing on the beaches. Rarely are the fishing rods and tackleboxes included when packing the car. As a result, a lot of family fun and good eating is overlooked.

Immediately after spawning, crappie do a bit of wandering just offshore from the areas where you may have caught them in springtime. The weather has not made a total commitment into the hot, sultry temperatures ahead. Just after the spawn, you must cover plenty of water in finding crappie for the stringer, as they move about with seemingly no objective. They don't stay in one place long. You can chase them around with your trolling motor and cast jigs in every direction, or "spider leg" poles armed with live minnows. Or you can sit along a creek channel and wait for them to come to you. They will, sooner or later.

But as the water temperature continues its climb in degrees, crappie begin a migration back out into the main lake or back to the deeper channels of the river. All crappie do not do this, as witnessed by the occasional one you can snag back in the shaded cuts and more shallow areas offering cool water around springs, etc. But the great majority of the crappie will move straight out into the middle of the lake and locate on the edge of the old river channel where they can find relief from the heat in deeper water. You'll almost *always* find the larger crappie there. Some of the finest crappie fishing action I have ever experienced was in open, deep water when the temperature was bouncing around the 100-degree mark.

The banner day came on a boiling hot August day without a cloud in the sky. I had arranged for Country Music star Helen Cornelius to meet me at the lake and do a few hours of crappie fishing for the cameras. Helen wasn't big on fishing, as her busy schedule simply didn't permit her the time to enjoy such things. She didn't know fish don't bite in the hot summer, so she agreed to come along to help me do an article for a magazine. I wasn't positive the fish would cooperate, either, but who would turn down such an opportunity.

Carl Hamilton and another good friend, Darryl Armstrong (who was the I&E Officer for LBL at the time), soon put us on crappie that kept the lid on the Igloo at half-mast most of the time. We caught fish constantly. I couldn't even enjoy looking at Helen's legs in those super short shorts for a few minutes without having to divert my attention to the tug on the other end of my line from a fat slab crappie! It was a banner day for fishing, and we caught enough crappie to feed the community twice.

Using the advantage of a good depthfinder, you can find the shoulder of the old river channel in a lake quickly and easily. Just head for open water and watch the flashes or bottom depth on the paper. When you see bottom depths drop sharply, you're in business! Probably the best place to fish for summer crappie is where the ancient river bank comes up from 40 or 50 feet in the channel to about 12 feet on the shoulder. In June, July and August, crappie will be along the drop-off somewhere between 10 and 30 feet below the surface. You can bet on it. As a bonus, there will

Most people think crappie don't bite in hot weather!

be several other species of fish in the same place willing to take your minnow or jig.

In a large lake, once you have located the old river channel, you will have literally *miles* of productive water to work. When you find crappie at a certain depth along the channel, you will find them pretty much at the same depth for the entire length of the channel in either directon. Head into the wind with your trolling motor and stay on the shoulder. If you could see underwater, you would be amazed at the numbers of fish down there!

The major part of the battle is over once you find the river channel out in the lake during hot weather. Crappie *will* be there. However, as you may imagine, every square inch of bottom will not be holding fat fillets for your freezer. As always, crappie prefer structure. Stump rows, brushpiles and various other types of cover which hold their prey are top producers. Find a gradual slope along the channel which has structure to offer, and you're in the right area. Your depthfinder can point out the bottom configuration as well as the brush on it. Such places are probably best marked with a floating buoy tossed off to the side, and the boat is moved around slowly as you work out the area.

"Bottom-bumping" the area with your double-hook rig filled with lively minnows is deadly under these circumstances. You must work the heavy sinker carefully and thoroughly in the structure. Present your bait slowly all along the slope to determine at what depth the crappie are holding. When you find the productive depth, you'll discover most fish in the general area are holding at pretty much the same distance below your boat hull.

Summer crappie are usually not as aggressive as those you take in springtime. You must employ a degree of patience in your technique. Instead of having the crappie smack your bait the minute it goes down like they often do in spring, you may be forced to "tease" the fish a bit in summer. Present your minnow or jig slowly and completely all around the structure. With the dual-hook rig, you can actually rub up and down on all sides of a stump until the fish takes the minnow. If he's down there, he'll take it sooner or later.

One true advantage of summer crappie fishing comes from the fact fish will cooperate at any time of day out on the deep river channel. Crappie are sensitive to bright sunlight and heat, so you may find them in sheltered or shaded places when the sun is really coming down. But the fish will take a bait pretty much 24 hours a day if you put it where they live. They aren't heavy, active feeders in summer, but if you work the deep drop-offs around the river channel carefully, you can catch a fine stringer almost at will. This means next time you plan a family vacation in the summer, you can spend the more pleasant parts of the day doing fun things anybody else enjoys. During the "dead" hot part of mid-day, anybody who wants to put on a sunbonnet can go to the deep parts of the lake and catch crappie for supper!

Truly avid crappie fishermen get wet, muddy and exhausted in winter months when the water is low. They put out brushpiles, stake beds, hay bales or even old bed springs to serve as fish attractors later when springtime comes around. Vacations are scheduled with great care to coincide with the "peak" of the annual spawning runs. Their "secret hotspots" are closely guarded with far less than brotherly love, and companions who may have helped with the construction are warned not to reveal locations of these places at all costs. Sometimes the warning is tempered with the threat of bodily harm.

Frequently, the spring fishing is excellent, and the anglers feel their efforts have paid off well. Typically, they put away their crappie fishing gear and await the return of fish to the shallows again next year. Unfortunately, they are missing some of the best action of all which takes place only a month or so later.

Several years back, Jack Savage and I did an article on his local waters in the Midwest. It was hot, still and muggy. Even at 6:00 a.m. when we

Author gets a hug from Helen Cornelius during summer crappie-fishing adventure.

met at the dock, the air felt heavy. We were in for some uncomfortable hours under a cloudless sky and we were going fishing for crappie. I made sure there was plenty of beer in the cooler.

We motored less than 1500 yards from the dock and Jack shut down the big engine. He made some mental calculations, lining up a couple of points on shore, and then flipped on the depth-finder. A couple of kicks with the trolling motor, and over went a floating marker bouy.

"You can start catching now, Buck," was his comment.

"That easy, huh?" I replied.

"Yep, this channel shoulder runs about a half-mile out towards that Coast Guard bouy, then it turns back and heads for that little island over there," he said, pointing somewhere off to the right. "We should pick up crappie all along here, except for a short stretch just before we get to the bouy."

Jack and I both used conventional fly rods and reels, the reels filled with heavy mono instead of fly line. On the business end of the outfit was the bottom-bumping rig.

On the very first drop, the guy came in with a double. A pair of pound-plus crappie went flopping into the ice chest, and our day of "lousy summer fishing" was off to a great start! During the three hours which followed, the temperature climbed steadily until it topped 90 degrees. The heat and glare on the water was making the beer disappear rapidly, and we were running low on minnows. The ice chest was practically full. We went back to the dock for either a late breakfast or early lunch. Then we cleaned and iced down 74 nice crappie before noon.

Summer crappie fishing can be a whole lot of fun.

Following the pattern of most dudes who write magazine articles for outdoor publications, I began to ask questions and scribble answers on my K-Mart tablet. The photographs were done, the fish were on ice, and now it was time to wind up business with a relaxed question-and-answer session sitting at a table in the air-conditioned restaurant at the resort. I made the mistake of assuming summer crappie could be caught best in the early and late hours of the day, and said so.

With a smile, my pal corrected my thinking, and said, "Come on, I'll show you."

Minutes later, we were back on the water for a hands-on demonstration. By this time the mercury had outdone itself; the large "Drink Coca-Cola" thermometer hanging in the shade on the boat dock displayed a shimmering 101-degree reading.

A few water skiers were buzzing around Jack's favorite drop-offs in open water, so he turned the boat slightly into shore and headed for a new spot.

"This place features a more drastic change in bottom depth," he began, "but the extremely shallow water here on top is filled with stumps and snags only inches beneath the surface. Skiers only come thru here once! I doubt we'll be bothered with them."

We began by bouncing our bait at 15 feet down the sharp drop-off, keeping the boat positioned over the shoulder with the trolling motor and depthfinder. That produced only a couple of fish in the mid-day sun, so we tried working a couple of feet deeper. That worked.

It was slow-going, and the action was less than furious. But we caught crappie in good numbers

In summertime, fish the old river channel out in the middle of the lake to find crappie.

and the fish were of good size. The drop-off selected sported plenty of snags and stumps, and judging from the depthfinder readings, it featured a "stair step" configuration with large or small ledges at different depths going down. It was necessary to put the minnows right next to the structure and leave them there motionless for a few seconds. If that didn't produce, the bait was moved up and down slowly, keeping the minnows almost touching the stump or snags. Usually, that would tease a fish into taking the present. We couldn't prove a definite pattern, but it appeared many of the crappie were holding on the shaded side of whatever structure we worked. The mid-day sun made shade scarce, regardless of which side the fish happened to like, but in cases where it was available, they usually took advantage of it.

The superior sense of "feel" you get when tight-lining on a light, sensitive pole with the lead weight below the hooks is a genuine benefit under these (and other) conditions. Had we been unable to "feel" the underwater structure, we would never have been able to entice large numbers of crappie with our bait, as we would have spent much of the time with our minnows positioned out and away from the structure instead of smack on it. Tight-lining is a very easy, simple procedure, and with a little practice you can become quite good at feeling stuff below the boat with the lead weight. You get to feel a lot of crappie on the end of the outfit, also.

Using this technique and working the 12-to-15-foot drop-offs in open water with the tight-line rigs, I have boated hundreds of good crappie while other fishermen stayed home in July and August. This has been done fishing at all hours of the day and night without noticing a material difference in success. Often, crappie bite best just before a storm comes thru the area. Fishing seems better when there is a light breeze across the water during daylight hours, and fishing in a light, steady drizzle of rain is absolutely excellent.

Summer crappie are not overly hard to please. They'll hit tiny jigs equally well as they do minnows. Sensitive "crappie" poles rigged with dual-hook tight-lining outfits are great producers, as are fly rods with the same type bottom hardware, or ultra-light outfits casting jigs or tiny spinners. Vertical jigging in structure along old river or creek channels pays off with real fun and tablefare, and you'll catch a wide variety of fish species.

Floating bouys or structure markers are quite helpful, especially when working along a channel edge or long point with drop-offs on one or both sides. You can even mark a particular stump or snag which yielded three or four crappie, returning to it a few minutes later to try for a couple more. If you're not familiar with an area of bottom, you can work it out with your depthfinder, tossing over markers along the channel edge as you go along. Once you have identified a reasonable stretch of the channel shoulder, all you have to do is head the boat into the wind and use your trolling motor to ease down the path between bouys, insuring your efforts remain in productive water. When you have reached the last bouy in the series, and if you caught fish on the first pass, motor back to the starting point and repeat the fun.

Catching "doubles" on the bottom-bumping rig is not uncommon.

When you discover an especially good spot in open water, take the time to line up some natural landmarks on shore so you can reposition the boat there again. *Write the info down* on a piece of paper so you don't forget. It's tough remembering a month later whether the water tower was supposed to be on the right or left side of the third telephone pole on the second bridge across from the white house with the funny-looking roof. Some of us have trouble remembering to put the plug in the boat before launching.

A slight rise in water level usually sparks fishing, and can be a tip-off providing valuable info on depth. Generally, a rise in water level will cause the fish to come up slightly in depth. A slight fall in water level will normally cause the fish to move slightly deeper down the slope. A cloudy day will cause the fish to come up in depth, also, even in August. (This is especially true in spring and fall crappie fishing.)

Fishermen talk a lot about water color when they return to the dock. Dingy water, even quite muddy water, will give up crappie in quantity. But the fisherman has to be more patient as he works his bait. Fish cannot see great distances in cloudy water, but they don't go on a fast as a result. Work your minnows or jigs slowly, remembering you must get the things within view of the fish before he can take it. Once the fish sees the bait, he likely will take it. Where legal, very small goldfish are great baits for dingy water. They live longer, are more active, and are more easily seen by a crappie with mud in his eyes.

One important thing to remember about caring for your fish after catching them in the summer months is to *keep them away from the water* on

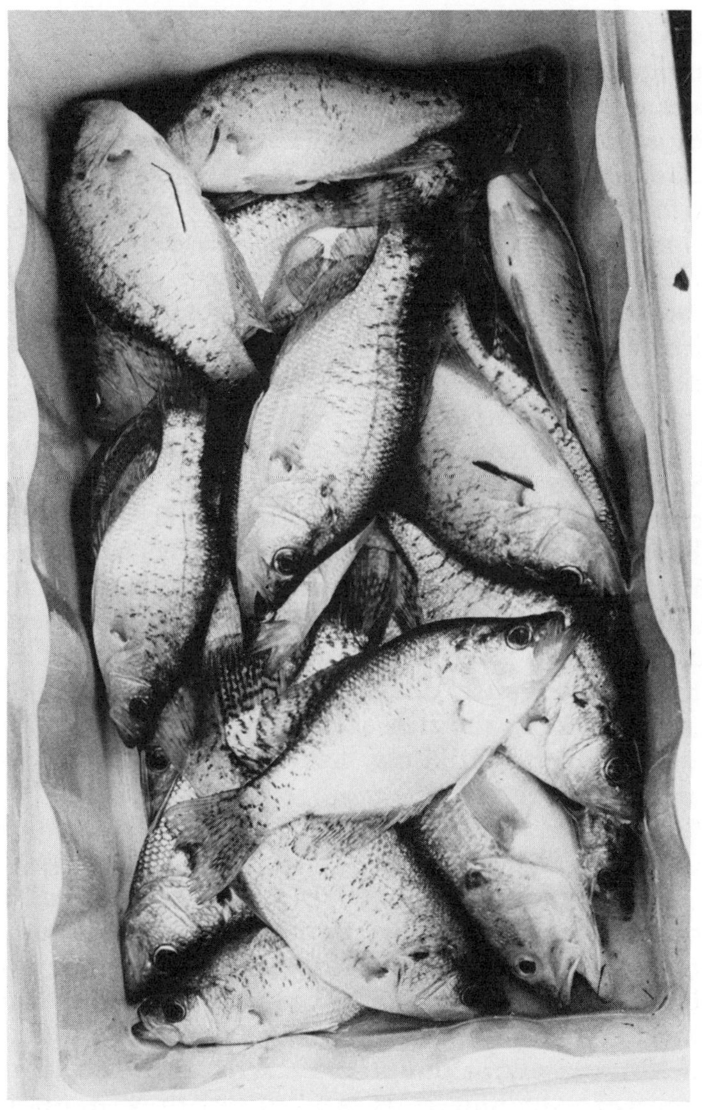

Especially in hot weather, keep your catch away from water in the ice chest on the way home if you don't want soggy fillets! (Photo courtesy TWRA)

the way home. While the crappie is alive and well, he goes about his business and has no problem keeping water from entering his flesh. I'm no biologist, so I can't explain the routine in scientific terms, but let's just say Mother Nature gives fish some kind of built-in mechanism which keeps water from soaking thru their scales and into their bodies. Once you capture the fish and kill it, those little "body pumps" stop working, and the fish will absorb water. This is why so many crappie fishermen are disappointed when they return home with soggy fillets.

In summertime, all fish have trouble living in your live well or on your stringer placed over the side. Heat and stress do them in quickly. You will have far better-tasting fish if you carry along an ice chest in the boat. Put the ice in the bottom, and lay a cloth towel on top of the ice. Fish are caught and tossed into the ice chest atop the towel. Frequently drain off the water from melted ice, and keep the fish away from that water. The result will be infinitely more firm, better-tasting tablefare.

As minnows are probably the most popular crappie bait these days nationwide, a few words on selection are in order. Most of us roar up impatiently to the boat dock, buy whatever the guy has in his tank, and rush out on the water with them. Unfortunately, a couple of hours later, the minnows are all dead, or at least so sick they produce no action on your hook.

Granted, if you fish in an area where there is only a single dock operator who peddles live minnows, you're going to be forced to live with whatever he has for sale. But if you have a choice, checking out the bait tank before plunking down your money can be fine insurance for better action later.

Look at the minnows in the tank. If they are the "fathead" variety (also known as "tuffies" and "chubs") the healthy ones should be swimming in a tight ball near the bottom of the tank, often in one corner. If they are loosely spread out all over the tank, or if they're swimming near the surface, the little guys are probably on their last leg and will die on you before you use the first dozen, especially if you don't have an aerated container to put them in.

Minnows which appear to be "climbing the wall" in the tank are also sick, especially the white sucker varieties which also should be swimming on or near bottom, although a bit more loosely balled together than fatheads. Common shiners ball loosely together when healthy, and do not go to the corner of the tank or swim around in it at random.

The pretty little Emerald shiners and the spottail variety require a great deal of oxygen to survive, and they cannot live with abrupt changes in water temperature. Two dozen of these in a standard minnow pail is about all you can keep alive. As the average minnow bucket holds about six quarts of water, you should limit the minnow population to some two dozen regular shinners, or three dozen fatheads. Keep the water temperature at 50 degrees or less. In summertime, this will mean using a fair amount of the ice in your drink cooler during the day, dropping a handful into the minnow pail frequently to keep the water cool for your bait.

Bob Maxwell unhooks nice crappie taken from shoreline brushpile on edge of drop-off.

The floating or sinking types of minnow buckets are fine in moderate weather where water temperatures in the lake are around 50 degrees. Keep the bucket filled with fresh lake water, dipped immediately prior to pulling in the removable half. This eliminates temperature shock when the minnows are pulled in from the lake water and placed into the bucket inside your boat. In hot weather, however, the surface temperatures of many lakes can hit 80 degrees, and dropping over a container into that hot liquid will effectively bake the minnows to death. Far better to keep the minnows in a bucket inside the boat and regularly add ice to the water where they swim. You'll need to change the water often also, keeping it fresh with oxygen. Do this gradually and at the time you add ice.

Oxygen tabs or a live well with a good aerator will help in keeping minnows alive under crowded conditions. If you purchase your minnows some distance away from the water, have the dealer package them in a large plastic bag filled with a shot of oxygen, and keep them out of direct sunlight and heat during the trip. When you get to the lake, place the bag overboard into the water unopened, allowing the water to temper itself, or keep the minnows inside your own aerated container with the initial water supply. Always add lake water gradually to avoid shocking the minnows. They don't catch nearly as many fish for you after they are dead.

Before you buy minnows, check out the dealer's holding tank. If it is poorly kept and dirty, take warning. If there are dead minnows floating around, the water is dirty or foamy, and the walls of the tank sport heavy iron deposits, you'll be better off spending your money on bait elsewhere. Bad odor around the bait tank is another tip-off to potential trouble.

If you fish often enough, it could be a good idea to construct a holding tank of your own at home. Minnows are rather easy to seine in most small creeks, and an old fiberglass tub, large garbage can or discarded bathtub can make a dandy place to keep your minnow supply. You'll need some form of aeration or a constant trickle of fresh water to keep the oxygen content adequate, and you cannot use city water because of all the chemical additives it contains which will kill the minnows. Having your own holding tank is well worth the time and effort needed to net the minnows locally, and saves money.

Fall

Both September and October are excellent months for catching crappie in good numbers. The trick is knowing where to find them, but it's not hard to accomplish.

During the summer, you should have been catching crappie out in the open water along the old channels and deeper drop-offs. As the autumn weather approaches, crappie migrate again. They leave the deeper waters around the river channel, moving inward toward shore. This time, they don't typically go all the way to the bank as they do in spring, but stop somewhere along the way where conditions appeal to them prior to the approaching winter months soon to follow.

There is a fair amount of controversy among fishermen in some of the Deep South states as to whether certain species of panfish spawn once a year or twice a year. While I have never caught a crappie in the fall which was filled with eggs, some anglers in Georgia and Florida swear they have done so. I do not dispute their word, but I'm willing to bet the fish never completed the full circle; ie: building nests, spawning and rearing the fry in fall. Some species of fish are indeed fall spawners. Not crappie.

Fall fishing success is a matter of knowing where to find the fish, employing basic techniques.

I think what happens may be a key to finding and catching crappie in the fall months. Remember we said fish are totally controlled and motivated by their environment. The list of various stimuli which affect them is long, but surely Numero Uno is water temperature. If 65 degrees happens to be the magic mark which triggers crappie in your area to spawn, you might consider your waters hit that temperature *twice* each year. Once in the spring when waters are warming up, and once *in fall when they are cooling down*.

As water temperatures cool after a hot summer, the fish react by moving toward shore. There may be several reasons for this, not the least of which is that their food supply probably does exactly the

A genuine "slab" crappie like this one puts up a dandy fight on light tackle!

same thing. The biological urge to reproduce may be sparked again as water temps move into the 65-degree range. However, opposite from the situation in the springtime, water stays in the optimum range only for a short period, then continues dropping. When the fish feel the water continuing to drop in degrees instead of climbing slightly, they react by shutting down the process of spawning, if indeed it was ever truly triggered into action.

Knowing crappie will be moving into more shallow waters from out in the lake where they spent the summer is helpful to your success. Now you can follow them in, keeping in mind they will travel natural underwater highways as they migrate. Your depthfinder makes it possible, as does a good topo map of the lake.

The majority of crappie fishermen believe their quarry comes to shore only once a year. They say crappie come to the shallows to find brush and stick-ups during their spawning runs, (which they obviously do) and during the remainder of the year, the fish scatter all over the lake in deep water. Not true.

In early and mid-fall, crappie head right back into the bays and creek mouths where you found them in March. They seek out the high spots, ridges, humps and underwater islands. Crappie will be schooled tightly in similar fashion to the way you find them just prior to their spawning. And you will find them located in basically the same places offshore.

Unlike in April and May, the fish will stay in these spots for much longer periods of time. Maybe for up to six weeks or two months. Later, a slight shift in location comes when the true winter temperatures arrive, and that shift is out a bit *away* from shore onto more extreme drop-offs. (We covered all that in the section on Winter.)

Fall crappie fishing is much easier than you may think. Practically every technique described earlier will work now, even including fishing under lanterns! As a true bonus, you will practically have the lake or river to yourself. Everybody else has either gone hunting or put away their fishing gear for the winter!

The phone rang at 6:00 a.m. and a cheerful voice on the other end tried to make its way thru the fog in my brain caused by a late-night date on the typewriter trying to make a deadline.

I finally realized the caller was a magazine editor who had overlooked the time difference between his city and mine, and who was asking me if I wanted to do an assignment for him on crappie fishing. Instinctively, I said something like "heck yes, I'll be delighted to do it for you." Then I hung up and went back to sleep.

A few hours later, after several cups of coffee, it dawned upon me what I had done. Magazine editors often forget little things like the season of the year when they make requests and assign deadlines. Here it was, late fall, and this guy wanted a full-blown article on catching spring crappie. He wanted it in two weeks so he could slot it into the advance work required in his office to make the April issue. You know, the one that always comes out in March but says April on the cover. This was all fine and dandy, except all the photos I had at the moment had already been used up in other articles on the subject, and editors are rather adamant about refusing to use photos which have previously appeared in other magazines. The "prove your success with photos" routine remained a requirement, but the real problem came to light when I looked out the window and watched the final few leaves on the trees falling to the frost-covered ground.

I flavored my next cup of coffee by mixing it with something from a brown bottle and reached for the phone, dialing the number of a drinking buddy of mine who lived on the other side of town.

"Doug, I'll pay you the twenty bucks I owe you if you'll go fishing with me this weekend," I began.

After much debate about my sanity, the fish not biting and my agreeing to replace the blade on his lawnmower I unfortunately introduced to some rocks in my front yard the summer before,

In the fall, crappie normally can be found around the same type structure as they were in early spring.

Doug reluctantly agreed. I didn't mention the photographs and how they would have to be taken.

Saturday mid-morning I pulled up in my friend's driveway, boat and gear in tow. After more discussion on the subject of frostbite and that last incident when we went fishing together and ran out of beer in August, Doug climbed into the pickup cab and we headed for the lake. I had to give him the twenty bucks first.

Minnows were purchased at the fourth place we tried. The launching ramp was deserted, except

Fresh-caught fish for supper cooked outdoors provides a real treat.

for a few unconcerned crows trying to warm themselves on the blacktop of the parking lot in the weak sunshine. We motored from the ramp out into the main lake, turned left and headed for Johnson Creek, the largest one entering the lake on that side. I drove the boat slowly to reduce the chill factor. Upon arrival we had a cup of my special pre-mix coffee, and that helped a bit.

Using the depthfinders, I found a couple of ridges whose tops were some 15 feet below the surface, marked them with floating bouys, and we began working the area. Doug had a couple of additional cups of the pre-mix and began warming up noticeably. By the time we had a dozen nice crappie in the boat, I figured he was about ready for the photo session.

"We need to pretend this is springtime," I explained carefully, filling his mug again. "I know it's not quite this chilly in April, but it only takes a few moments to focus and shoot this little camera."

I agreed to help him cut and haul two loads of firewood to his house before he agreed to remove his gloves and heavy coat. He even rolled up his sleeves and put on the lightweight cap with the Berkley Trilene emblem on it as I requested. Being careful to avoid getting any of the bleak, leaf-forsaken trees along the shore into the photos, I composed the pictures in the viewfinder of the camera to crop out his heavy insulated boots and the cup of pre-mix. For all practical purposes, the resulting photos looked like we were catching early spring crappie!

Freelance outdoor writers are a devious bunch. That article, with accompanying photos, appeared in an April issue of a largely-circulated magazine in 1980. Please forgive the deceit, but knowing where the crappie could be caught in late fall made it all possible to do on time for the deadline!

If you enjoyed good crappie action during the spring spawning runs, return to the same general areas to catch fish in the fall. Just go offshore a bit further in your search. Use your sonar unit to pinpoint underwater ridges and humps. There is little question (actually no question at all) you will find crappie on that structure if they were there in the spring. These places are used as concentration points in both spring and fall.

If you're fishing new waters and are unfamiliar with the area, purchase a topo map. Study it until you find high points in the bays or creek mouths. Then go there and use your depthfinder to zero in on target.

Once you locate these concentration points, there are several productive ways to fish for crappie. A common method with live bait is to "spider leg" your boat with several poles and drift across the area slowly. When the crappie show interest in your offerings, pitch out a marker bouy. Continue drifting a while, dropping additional bouys as indicated by the action. Perhaps an hour of this routine should produce a definite pattern. You can spend the remainer of your time using the trolling motor to work the bouys one at a time, or use the sonar to evolve the ingredients the fish want in the way of depth and structure. Then motor around easily, fishing each time the needed requirements are found.

Tiny jigs can be cast in "shotgun" fashion all around the area and retrieved slowly back to the

Carl Hamilton demonstrates effectiveness of his open-water technique. (Photo courtesy Kentucky Tourism)

boat, or "danced" along near bottom. Fall crappie will take a jig with equal enthusiasm as they will minnows. And you can cover more territory by casting in all directions as you drift. If you're "meat fishing" as I sometimes do, you can use a combo of baited poles stuck into rod holders on the gunnels, and cast jigs as you drift!

Once again, the double-hook, tight-line rig is an excellent choice for fall crappie catching. The magic of having two hooks in the water at different depths gives you a genuine advantage in finding the productive zone. Bottom-bouncing up and down the sides of those ridges can and will produce fall crappie. Crappie are not notorious for chasing a bait like bass. Neither will they actively change depth either up or down to smack a minnow unless they have missed the dinner bell a couple of days running. Put a nice, lively minnow under one's nose, and he'll usually take it anytime of the day, however. But don't count on having him get excited over a bait placed two or three feet away from him in the fall months. The double-hook rig simply increases your chances of getting the minnow at the exact depth where the fish's mouth happens to be waiting. Makes a big difference.

As the water continues to cool in the later part of October or thereabouts, crappie often take a final crack at hitting the banks for a very brief time. It's almost as if they have been frustrated by the reverse water temperature trends, and just want to check out things along shore to be sure they really don't get to spawn this time! I haven't seen them go back into the ends of bays or coves at this time, but they indeed will go to very shallow water along the creek mouths and larger bays. You can catch them there handily for a week or two, often in three or four-foot water. After this short flurry of shallow-water action, the crappie move to their wintering real estate to homestead until spring.

The tag end of fall months finds crappie moved out a bit into deeper waters of the lake. As covered in the section on Winter, your best bet is to find places where the bottom offers a combination of deep and shallow water. Long slopes or drops featuring shallow water at the top end, and very deep water at the other, are almost sure bets for late fall crappie. A slope which goes from 5 feet down to 40 feet would be ideal. All you have to do is work the different depths until you hit it right.

Once again, as the water gets cooler, the crappie's body metabolism slows down. You'll need sensitive tackle and patience. Use smaller minnows or jigs.

Fall crappie anglers should be prepared to move and change techniques rapidly and often. Flexibility is the key. It may be 70 degrees and sunny one day, spitting sleet the next. Fall weather typically changes quickly, often going from one extreme to the other. Fish are going to move with the weather changes. To catch them, you have to move when they do.

Because of that very brief movement into shallow water just prior to their migration into deeper haunts, many fishermen continue trying for them in the shallows. You can still pick up a straggler or two there sometimes, but basically you're working in the wrong areas by staying shallow all the time.

It cost me a case of beer to learn that lesson many years ago. I had been working on a magazine article for two or three days in late October, catching crappie in limited numbers in five-foot water near a point going out into the lake. I was staying with a good friend, Bob Maxwell, in Grand Rivers, Kentucky. Bob is one of the more knowledgeable hunters and fishermen I have ever worked with, but he was busy at his job and couldn't get away to join me on the lake.

Each night I would return to the house and we would discuss the day's activity with minnows and jigs. Each night, Bob would listen to my tales of slow and limited success, and then tactfully suggest I try moving out into deeper water along the same point. I would nod in agreement, but not follow through the following day. There have

Getting your jig to the right depth and working it at the right speed produces handily. (Photo courtesy TWRA)

The crappie angler who is willing to change methods and experiment is the one who gets the results. (Photo courtesy Tennessee Wildlife Resources Agency)

been other times in my life when I may have been equally stubborn on a subject, but I can't recall them. After all, crappie are a schooling species, and I *was* catching a few in the shallows.

The third night's discussion followed the set pattern. When asked if I had tried the deeper area of the drop, my response brought a chuckle and a challenge.

"If you weren't so bull-headed, you'd have a boatload of crappie by now!" Bob teased. "I've got a couple of hours in the morning free, and I'll bet I can catch more crappie in your spot in one hour of fishing than you caught all day!"

I took the bet. And lost.

It was so simple I couldn't believe it. Bob sat in the bow and worked the trolling motor. He began working the shallow area where I had spent three days, then moved and changed gradually as he covered deeper and deeper water on the drop-off. About 30 yards from where I had wasted as many hours fishing shallow, he dropped over a marker bouy into 16-foot water. This he did after bringing in four straight slab crappie while holding the boat there with the trolling motor.

Bob grinned widely as he invited me to share in the fun, which I did immediately. (I ain't *that* stubborn!) We proceeded to haul in over 30 nice crappie in the remaining 45 minutes before Bob had to return to work.

By way of consolation, Bob indicated the crappie *could* have been shallow when we arrived, as they often feed up a slope when their food supply moves there during the day. It just happened I had missed that feeding movement previously. *Searching, moving and changing depth is the key to success in crappie fishing.*

Getting into a rut and refusing to alter your approach can be costly.

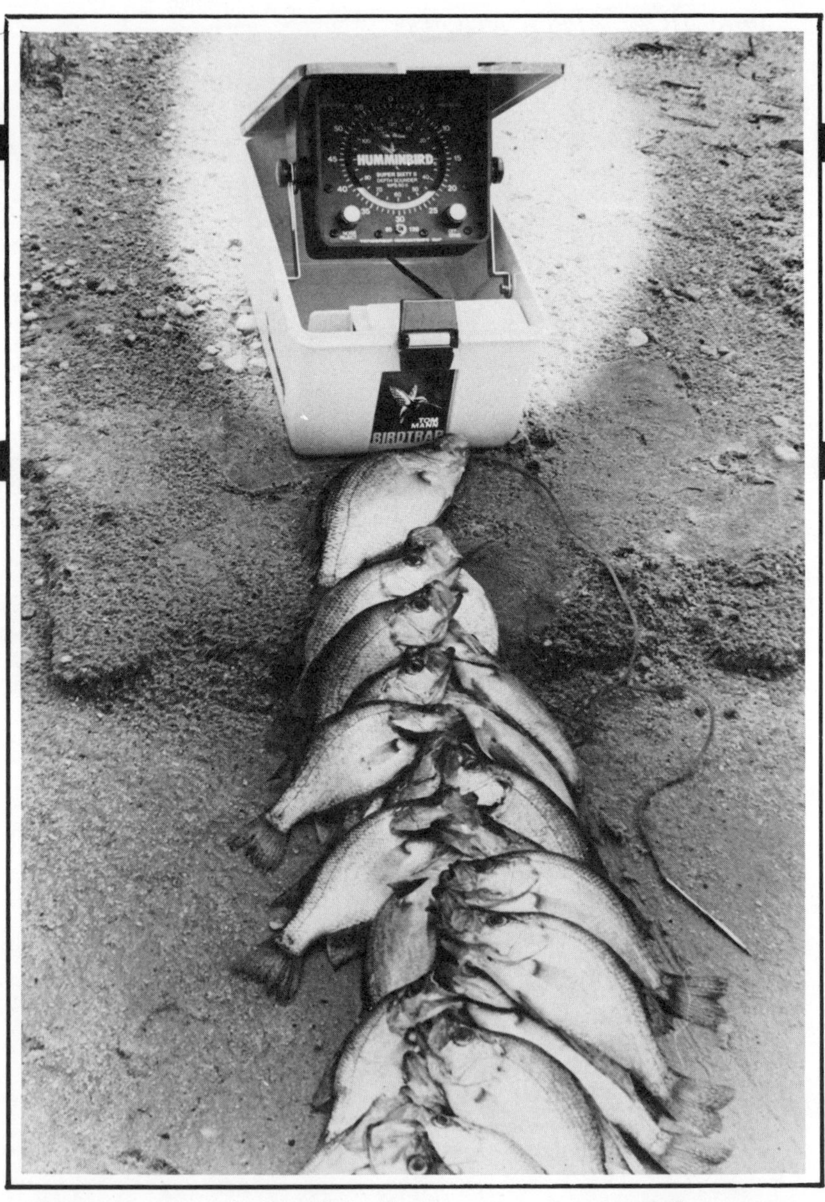

Proper use of depthfinders is to successful crappie fishing what flour is to hot biscuits! (Photo courtesy John Phillips)

6

Fishing With 12 Volts

Few species of fish lend themselves better to the effective use of depthfinders than do crappie. Learning the general areas the fish will be using at various times during the year is essential. Once that is mastered, your ability to put your bait within eating distance of a crappie comes from expertise with sonar. You can fish half a day within only a few yards of these fish when they are not active, and come home without a bite. Depthfinders allow you to eliminate that critical small distance which sometimes makes the difference between filling your cooler with fillets and sitting on top of it watching a motionless cork float.

You don't have to be a professional fisherman to use your sonar unit like one. You *do* have to experiment and learn from both your successes and your mistakes. Crappie move about in the lake or river during the year with genuine predictability. You can use your depthfinder to follow those movements and migrations effectively. The trick is knowing the patterns crappie follow, and being able to interpret what your sonar is telling you when it blinks, flashes or draws funny-looking pictures on paper.

Spending time on the water with your depthfinder is the best way to learn. But you have to work at it. Simply staring at the thing like it was a TV set won't improve your knowledge any more than staring at a TV set! You have to experiment, take notes, and most of all, analyze the results.

When you find what you feel is good structure on the sonar machine, and then prove this true by catching fish, make a note of how the readings looked. I know this is asking a lot, as most of us go to the water to have fun, not to take notes. But in the long run, you'll be far better off on the following trips. Once you figure it out, you can use that knowledge to repeat the fun and success again and again. It's called "paying dues" in some circles. And called a pain in the behind by those who know just enough about sonar interpretation to think they are about ready to enter the pro circuit, if only they could catch more fish regularly.

Your depthfinder neither attracts fish nor creates hunger pains in their stomachs. It merely tells you where the fish are living. And where they are not. You already know crappie are very structure-oriented, and after reading the preceeding chapters, you have a good idea of what type structure they will prefer in each month of the year. So your job becomes one of finding the appropriate structure at the appropriate depth. Once found with the depthfinder, you can bet crappie will be present. It's *almost* automatic. You can pinpoint their wet little noses practically every time out.

The following illustrations are taken from chart paper I have burned on various lakes using a graph depthfinder. These are actual readings, so forgive some of the excess images which appear on the paper not directly related to crappie fishing. I guess some of the other fish in the lakes wanted their picture taken, too.

Graph paper is used for illustrations because it is so much easier to read and understand. Taking a picture of a working flasher can present mechanical problems, too. The rate of flash sometimes allows the camera shutter to miss the action, especially on bright days when a fast shutter speed must be used. There are comments with each chart paper illustration which describe how the situation would look on your flasher.

Ridges, humps, ledges and drop-offs with structure, are all ideal places to find crappie year-round. All you need to know is the correct depth.

Graph paper #1

The bottom is almost blanketed with crappie and the paper was run during the spawning season! As you can see, all crappie don't spawn at the same time. All during the several weeks when conditions are right, crappie are coming and going to and from the banks. If you will back off away from shore a bit, you'll probably find areas like this where the action can be super hot. The wad of fish suspended on the left is a school of shad.

Crappie holding near the bottom will appear as multiple signals on your flasher *above* the primary bottom reading. You will have to look closely to spot the small changes in readings when the fish are holding this close to bottom. The school of shad will be a wide signal covering several feet on unit's face. Disregard them and get that bait to the bottom!

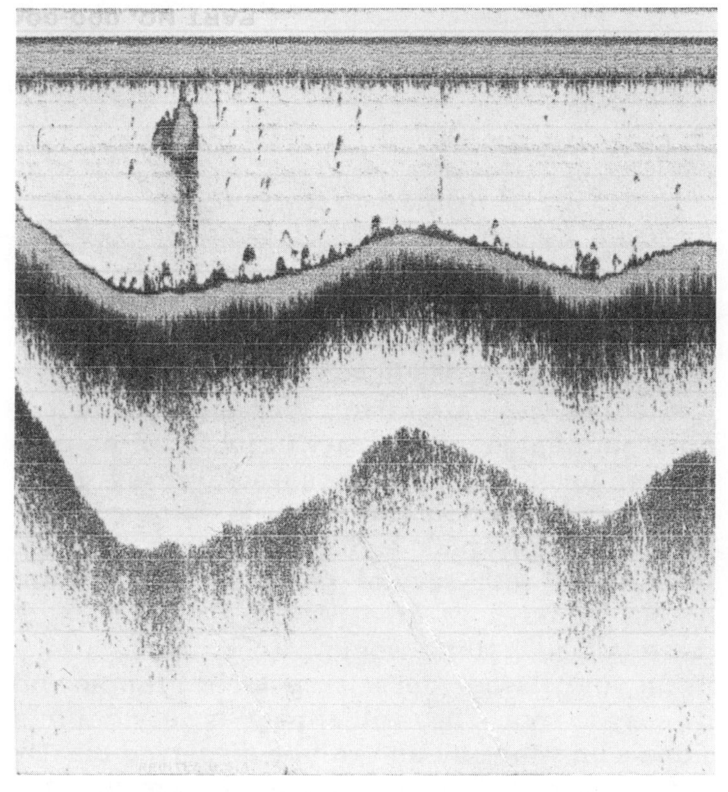

Graph paper #2

Sometimes crappie like to suspend off bottom a few feet as these are doing. Working your bait at different depths is necessary in locating the productive level for them. Guys who always fish the same way (on bottom, for example) often miss the fish when they pick a different depth to hold. Driftfishing with several poles out at different depths would be a great way to find and catch these fellas. Trolling would produce well, also.

On your flasher, these suspended crappie will be easy to spot. They will appear as very definite signals on your unit and will be displayed clearly above the main bottom reading you are getting. For easy fishing, note the distance on your flasher between the fish signals and the bottom reading; drop your bait over and allow it to fall to the bottom. Then reel up the distance noted between fish and bottom. Your minnow or jig will then be smack in front of their noses.

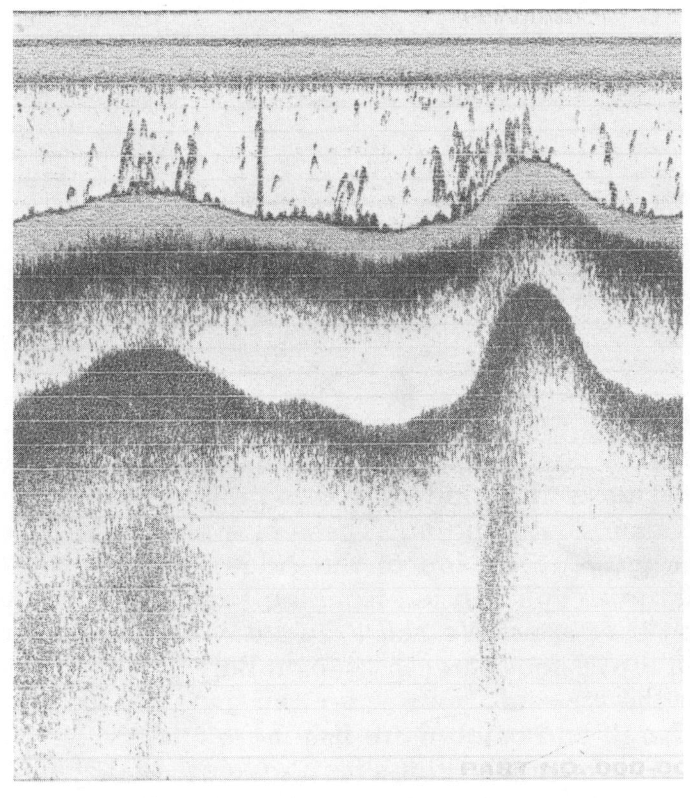

Graph paper #3

This is the kind of concentration most of us dream about finding! These crappie are feeding actively up on top of the ridge, and are quite large as you can tell from the size of the images on the paper. We had a field day catching them in the 20-foot water in June on Barkley Lake. This is the type info your sonar can generate for you. Use it, and catch more fish more often.

This particular ridge features a gradual change in the bottom depth, so fish signals will appear as distinct images holding on or near bottom. You should find your flasher will pick them up easily as "new" signals with a definite space between the bottom signal and the readings coming back from the fish.

Graph paper #4

Crappie relate closely to various types of structure. Here, they are holding between two underwater brush piles placed there by obliging fishermen several months before. The fishermen chose to sink their artificial fish attractors near the end of a point going out where a small creek entered the river. A natural route for migrating crappie to follow, the spot was noticed and occupied by numerous fish most of the year.

Both brushpiles will appear on your flasher as sudden changes in bottom depth. The fish holding around them will be seen as additional "blips" or flashes on the face of your unit. Finding these underwater changes in depth, coupled with the extra signals from fish, means it's time to drop over a marker and get down to work.

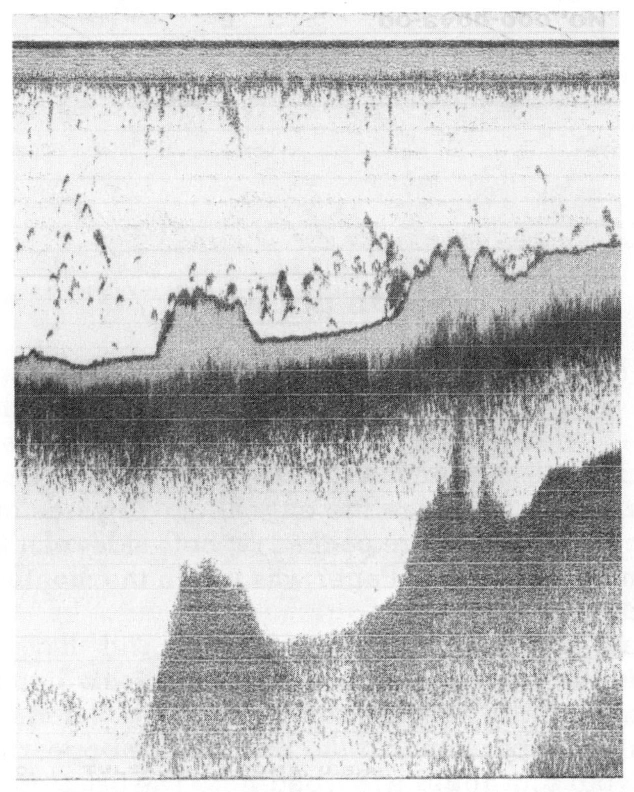

Graph paper #5

In both early spring and late fall, crappie will move to underwater humps or ridges like this one. Once found, they will provide plenty of action on jigs or minnows. This particular ridge ran parallel to the shoreline only about 75 yards offshore. Crappie were packed on both sides of it for almost a half-mile! Paper was run in the month of October.

In this situation, your flasher will have a definite tendency to overlook the fish. Signals coming back from the somewhat steep change in bottom depth beneath the boat will be appearing on your unit as multiple readings. The fish signals often become lost among those multiple bottom readings. Due to the mechanics of a sonar unit, there is very little you can do to help the situation. In the fall, just find the ridges and underwater humps, then fish them carefully. Crappie will be there.

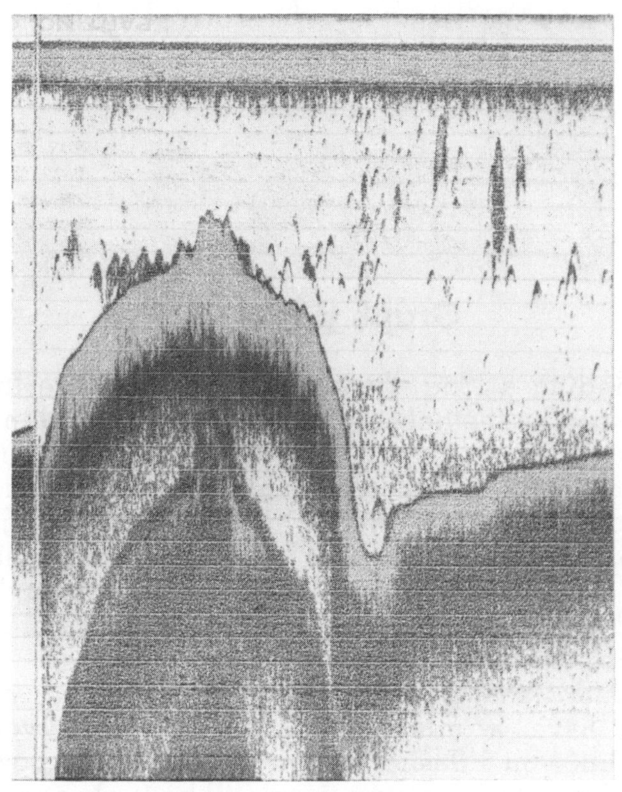

Graph paper #6

Finding a long, gently-sloping point like this one can be the ticket to fantastic crappie fishing. Work the point from the shoreline out, using almost any of the techniques and methods described earlier. When you find the magic depth, you're all set for a great time. Points like this are excellent places to look for crappie in the fall, and also are great places to do business under the lanterns at night in mild weather.

As this change in bottom depth is gradual, you will have a minimum of distortion in your readings on a flasher as you proceed up or down the slope. Fish holding there will be fairly easy to spot, and will appear as separate images on or near the bottom. They will appear quickly as you pass over if the fish are schooled tightly, and you may need to toss out a marker bouy for reference in positioning the boat as you come back to the spot.

Graph paper #7

In the hot summer months, crappie head for the old river channel out in the lake, where they take up residence somewhere along the shoulder. These fish are holding on a "step" or ledge on the shoulder of the channel in about 27-foot water. This paper was burned in the middle of the day in August, and once we found the fish, we caught them handily. The larger fish strung out across channel above the crappie are small stripers.

Your flasher will indicate the changing bottom depth by displaying multiple bottom readings as you proceed down the drop. When you pass over a "step" in the bottom configuration, your bottom readings will stabilize a bit, and fish signals should be apparent as images holding distinctly above bottom a foot or so. If the "step" or ledge is small in width, you may not be able to see the fish signals at all. Fish the area in confidence, however. Summer crappie are going to be there!

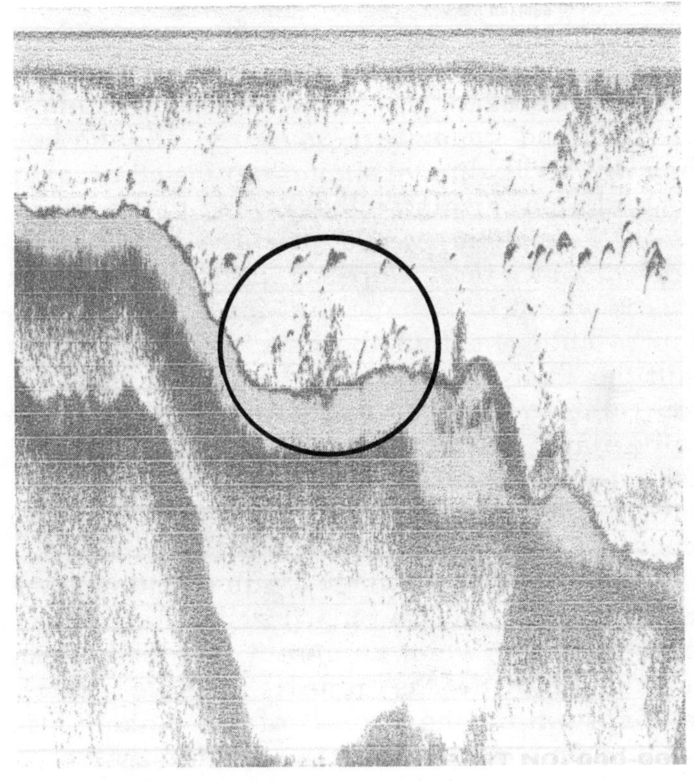

Graph paper #8

Here's an excellent example of how crappie will be found *somewhere* on a drop-off, and how they will be holding at similar depths all over the general area. Fishing either on top of the hump, or on the bottom, would produce little action. *Halfway* down these slopes is where the action is! This is why it is so important for you to change depths until you find the fish. Bottom-bumping with the dual-hook rig would find these fish for you rather quickly as you carefully worked the bait up and down the drop. During the day the fish may move either up or down the slope a bit, but this is an almost perfect picture of why you must find the productive zone to be successful.

Drop-offs present a truly tough situation when trying to discover fish on a flasher. You will see multiple flashes which represent only the bottom, as changing depths reflect multiple bottom readings within the "cone" of the signal. Fish holding on a drop-off can be spotted by the increased signal activity at a particular depth which remain somewhat constant as you proceed down the drop. It takes a keen eye and some experience to note this type action. At best, it's quite hard to do. Your best bet with a flasher is to find the structure and fish it in hopes the fish are there.

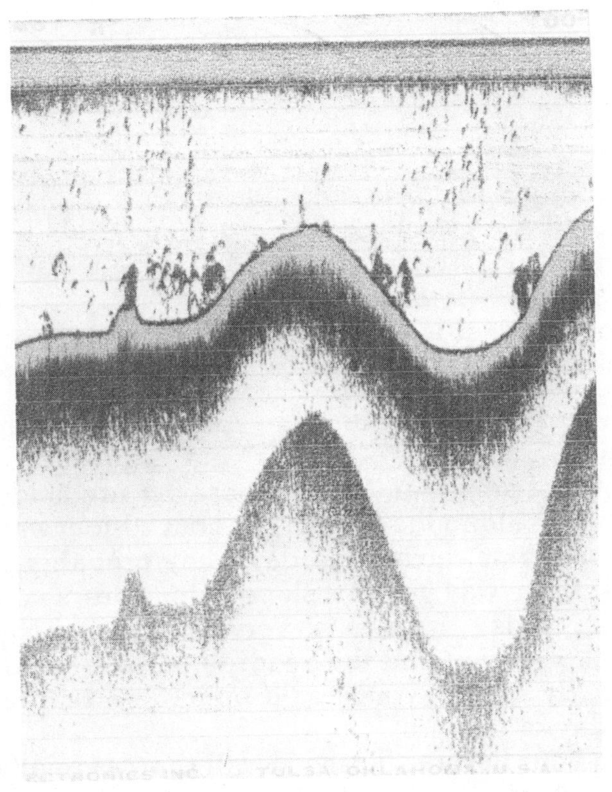

Graph paper #9

In early spring before the spawn, crappie mill around underwater islands and ridges in the mouths of creeks and bays. These fish are holding in stumps along the bottom in about 20-foot water. At some time during the day, they probably will work their way up the slope into more shallow levels. This group is very tightly schooled together. If you find this reading on your sonar in the early spring, you should be in for a real banner day of fishing!

On your flasher, these fish will show as relatively constant signals a foot or so above the main bottom reading. There will be a definite space between bottom and fish readings, as the fish are holding slightly above the bottom. This signal will change almost constantly, frequently merging into the bottom reading, as the fish are dispersed over several feet of depth.

Graph paper #10

There it is! We've found a pair of cedar Christmas trees sunk in about 20-foot water on the side of an underwater hump. The tops of the trees are totally covered up with crappie! Crappie will follow that ridge (lengthwise) in their natural movements throughout most of the year, and large numbers of them will stop there to feed when either coming or going. It's an ideal place to sink a tree-top, and as you can see from the fish holding there, a very productive one.

On your flasher, the signals from the tree will merge completely with the fish signals. Turn *down* the sensitivity on your unit and the tree will fade away materially, leaving the stronger signals from fish plainly to be seen.

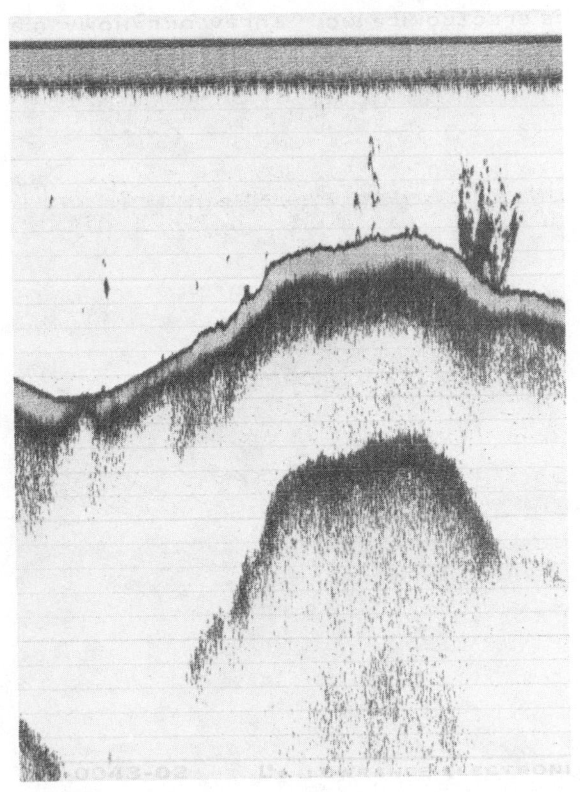

The eatin's almost as much fun as the catchin'! (Photo courtesy The Coleman Company)

Cleaning and Cooking

All you need to clean a nice mess of crappie is two beers, a knife and a spoon. If you're a non-drinker, save the beer for the cooking process later (the small amount of alcohol cooks out quickly, leaving a delicious flavor from the other ingredients).

A couple of things make fish-cleaning much easier. Start with a *spoon* for removing scales. I scraped the things with a knife for years, doing a half-way job, until a friend in Miami told me about the ease with which a *large spoon* does the trick. It's about three times as fast!

The next consideration is how and where to apply the knife for removing the head and entrails. This too, is both fast and easy. Scale your fish from tail to head, using the spoon to get even the hard-to-flip scales along the fins. You can skip scaling the part of the fish over the rib cage with this method; you're going to cut that away for the cats, anyhow.

After scaling, turn the fish upside-down (belly up) and place the knife blade between the vent and the bottom fin. Slice downwards until you hit the backbone. Then turn the knife blade towards the head and cut thru the ribs along the backbone until you reach the gills. There is a nice bite of meat atop the crappie's head, so angle the blade again, this time cutting from the backbone behind the gills slightly forward and around the head.

With a bit of practice, you can make the entire "stairstep" cut in almost one motion, effectively removing head, entrails and rib bones in one sweep. The tiny amount of meat lost in removing the rib cage is truly not worth the aggravation later trying to pick out the bones. And the speed of cleaning fish this way is well worth the loss, and then some!

Due to the size of the crappie's tail, and the slick coating of "swim juice" they have, I usually cut off the tail about a half-inch forward of the end. That tail takes up a lot of room in the skillet, and requires a lot of extra grease!

On larger crappie, be sure to use the knife blade to cut or "score" a path along the backbone from head to tail. This slit in the meat allows the hot grease to penetrate down to the backbone, completely cooking the fish into the center, and eliminates the unpleasant, sticky substance sometimes found there with only partially-cooked whole fish. Note this speeds cooking time, also.

When you hit the mark on "jumbo size" crappie, take time to fillet them. Boneless crappie fillets are a genuine treat. I grew up in the Deep South were folks take a big mouthfull of watermelon, mouth it a moment and spit the seeds skillfully. I can do pretty much the same with fish and fishbones. However, a select fillet of boneless

Using the method described, it'll take about 20 seconds per fish to convert this stringer into skillet-ready eating! (Photo courtesy Santee Cooper Country)

fish is still a joy on the table. Due to the texture of crappie meat, I don't remove the skin; otherwise, it may fall apart in the skillet. Even when cooking whole crappie, I like to remove the top and bottom fins before cooking if they are fairly large.

If you catch more fish than the night's supper table will require, and don't particularly feel like inviting in the neighbors, you'll need to freeze the surplus. Do it by placing the cleaned fish (or fillets) into milk cartons, either plastic or paper. All you do is fill the container to within an inch or so of the top and add water to the brim. The water obviously freezes, as do the fish, and you have almost perfect insulation for your catch: no freezer burn thru the frozen water. When you thaw your catch for a later meal, the taste is well preserved, and you can tell a material difference in flavor as opposed to freezing them in plastic bags or other containers without water. Freezers sometimes get hungry and eat the top layer of water in open containers, thus exposing your fillets, so you might be wise to close down the top of the milk cartons, or at least add an extra couple of inches of water above the meat.

Cooking crappie is quite simple. Frying them in hot grease is probably the most popular method, as these fish do not lend themselves to exotic treatment in fancy steamers and servings accompanied by expensive herbs and foreign spices. Basically, crappie are "down home" tablefare, served with hushpuppies, coleslaw, french fries and/or fried onion rings. If you like a little extra flair to your fish-frying fun, you might serve up some fried green tomatoes on a side platter.

Outdoor fish fries are delightful in pleasant

Try cooking your fish on the balcony over a propane stove in the bottom of a turkey roasting pan. No odor in the house!

weather, and truly eliminate most of the clean-up chores afterwards. There are some excellent deep-fry cookers on the market which run off a 20-gallon propane tank and have a large basket for holding the fish, draining, etc. You may have a two or three-burner camping stove at home, too. If so, use the bottom half of a turkey roasting pan for the grease and goodies, place over the burners and watch the temperature carefully. Works fine.

If you're lucky enough to have the leisure of fishing and camping overnight, you will surely want to cook part of your catch on the lake or river bank. The texture of crappie meat doesn't make it very suitable for cooking over an open

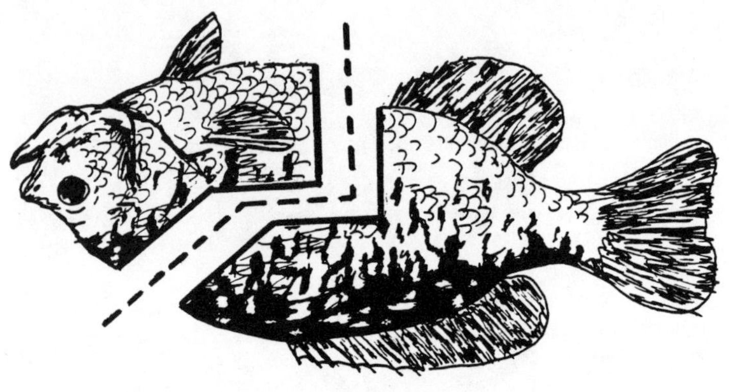

Proper line of cut for "speed cleaning" crappie.

fire impaled on a stick, but any number of other methods are quite successful. You can grill them (be sure to baste often with melted butter), wrap inside foil with butter and onion (or lemon) slices, or cook in a skillet with grease. If using grease in the skillet over an open fire, be careful to avoid a spill which can result in a dangerous flare-up. (Open fire fish-cooking in deep fat is best done by using a deep container like a Dutch oven without the lid.)

If you have the choice, try cooking your fish outside. Besides reducing the clean-up efforts later, you don't generate cooking odors in the house. Then too, there's something extra nice about the flavor of things cooked in the open air.

Here are a number of simple and easy recipes to enjoy.

Home Style Crappie

Salt and roll fish in cornmeal. (It's easier if you pour the salt and cornmeal into a paper sack, add fish and shake well until the fish are coated.) Deep fry the fish in oil or grease preheated to about 400 degrees. Oil should be deeper in the container than the thickness of the fish. Cook from nine to twelve minutes, depending upon size of fish. Drain well and serve hot.

Fried Onion Rings

Slice onions into thin rings. Soak in water with two or three teaspoons of sugar mixed and dissolved in.

Mix together one cup of flour, two tablespoons of salad oil, ¼ teaspoon of salt and ⅔ cup of water. Then beat the white of one egg until fluffy and add to the above mix. Drain the onion rings, pat dry and dip into the batter. Fry in hot deep fat until golden brown.

Old South Coleslaw

Take one head of cabbage, two carrots and one medium onion; grate into container and add sweet pickle relish and coleslaw dressing to suit your tastes. Mix well.

Hushpuppies Delight

1½ cups yellow cornmeal (not self-rising)
½ cup self-rising flour
1 onion, chopped
½ teaspoon salt
½ teaspoon baking powder
1 egg (break yolk, don't whip)
1 cup milk

Mix all ingredients together into a batter of fairly stiff texture. Use a tablespoon to dip one "ball" of batter at a time into pre-heated oil about 350 degrees. If you dip the spoon into a glass of water after each drop into the grease, it will make successive drops easier. Cook until hushpuppies are golden brown. Makes about 30 hushpuppies.

Fried Green Tomatoes

Cut firm green tomatoes into ¼ inch slices. Mix cornmeal with a generous amount of salt and a dash of sugar, then roll slices in mixture until well coated. Fry in bacon drippings or oil until brown. Turn only once while cooking.

Baked Crappie Pronto

Remove tails and fins from cleaned fish, score sides with knife blade. (Fillets work fine in this recipe also.) Place in skillet or flat pan with sides. Add small amount of water to prevent sticking.

Place pats of butter on top of each fish, sprinkle with salt and top with a slice of lemon. Cover with a lid and bake on 350 degrees for about six minutes. Remove lid and set oven to Broil. Cook for about two minutes, or until butter begins to turn brown. Serve with melted butter and lemon juice.

Beer Batter Fillets

Mix self-rising flour, egg and beer into a soupy batter. (Begin with two cups of flour and add other ingredients until finding the desired consistency.) Dip fillets into the batter and drop into pre-heated oil or grease sufficiently deep in the container to cover the fillets completely. These cook quickly, so be careful!

CREDITS

Art Direction
Jessica Jenkins

Art Production
Goodgraphiks
Nashville, Tennessee
Kaye Nicol, Production Assistant

Illustrations
Nancy Walsh

Typography
Ligature Typesetting Services
Nashville, Tennessee
Linda Bennie, Typographer

Copy Proofing
Jerrie Ingram

Printing
Harris Press, Inc.
Nashville, Tennessee

Additional copies of this book available from
**Outdoor Skills Bookshelf
P.O. Box 111501
Nashville, Tennessee 37211**

Learn to *Use Your* Depthfinder Like A Pro!

Author Buck Taylor has produced a book now being acclaimed by the experts as the most authoritative text available on the subject of using depthfinders effectively in your fishing. He takes a complicated subject and makes it easy to understand, forgetting the electronic circuitry jargon and concentrating on *proper use of your machine.*

Covering the effective ways to use your sonar machine in a straight-forward, "A to Z" approach, this book carries a money-back guarantee if you're not satisfied. IT'S THAT GOOD! Beginner or experienced sonar user, we promise you'll learn plenty from this outstanding presentation.

Fully illustrated with actual examples taken from sonar readings, there's absolutely no guesswork. Praised by professional fishermen and nationally-known outdoor journalists alike, Taylor's depthfinder book is fast becoming the "Bible" for sonar users. It is "must reading" for all who use depthfinders in their fishing endeavours.

Selection, Installation, Reading, Interpretation, Practical Application of your Knowledge to a variety of fish species, and Maintenance/ Troubleshooting are all covered in genuine detail. Often humorous, always taking the "no-nonsense" approach, Taylor has written the very best book on depthfinders we have ever read anywhere.

Reprinted by overwhelming demand, this book is yours for only $10.95, Postage Paid. Orders from outside the United States add $2.50. Residents of Tennessee add 6% State Sales Tax.

Do Not Miss This Opportunity To Increase Your Effectiveness and Success with your Depthfinder
(Regardless of brand name).

Order Today and Start Catching More Fish By Using Your Sonar Equipment to its Full Potential

Send check or Money Order to:

OUTDOOR SKILLS BOOKSHELF
P.O. Box 111501
Nashville, TN 37211